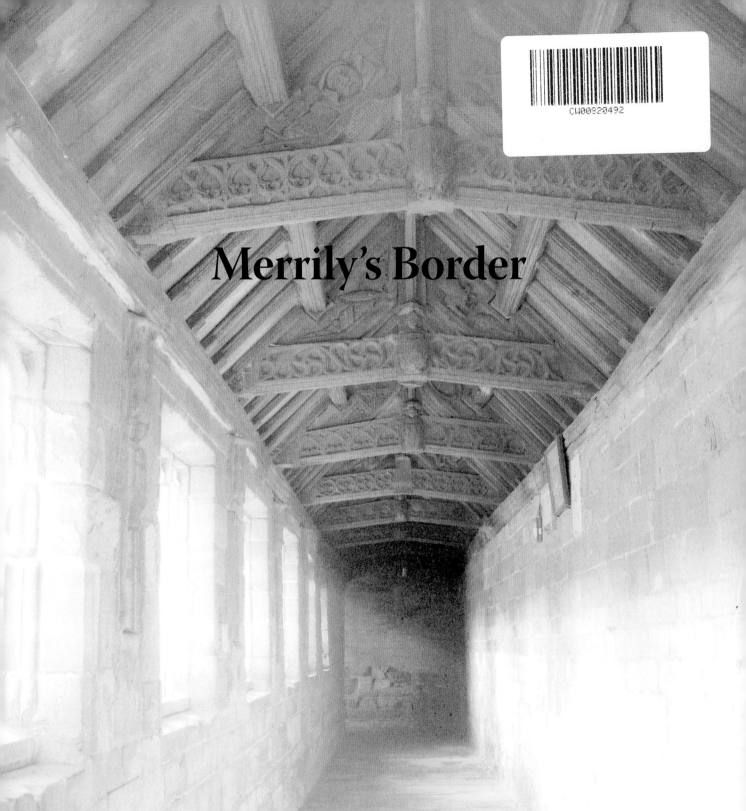

Merrily's Border

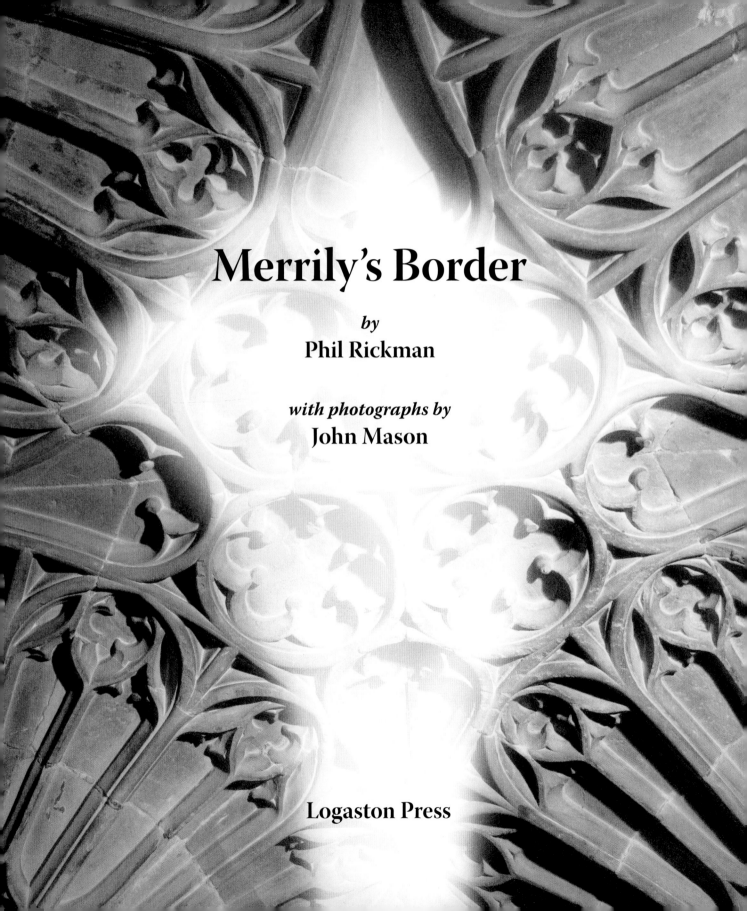

Merrily's Border

by
Phil Rickman

with photographs by
John Mason

Logaston Press

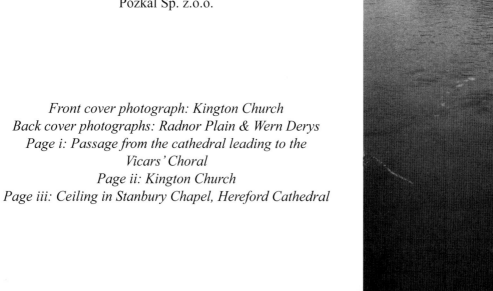

LOGASTON PRESS
Little Logaston Woonton Almeley
Herefordshire HR3 6QH
www.logastonpress.co.uk

First published by Logaston Press 2009
This edition published 2013
Copyright text © Phil Rickman 2013
www.philrickman.co.uk
Copyright illustrations © as acknowledged 2013

978 1 906663 69 8

Typeset by Logaston Press
and printed and bound in Poland
Pozkal Sp. z.o.o.

Front cover photograph: Kington Church
Back cover photographs: Radnor Plain & Wern Derys
Page i: Passage from the cathedral leading to the
Vicars' Choral
Page ii: Kington Church
Page iii: Ceiling in Stanbury Chapel, Hereford Cathedral

Eardisland

Contents

*Altar and reredos,
St Laurence's Church, Ludlow*

Acknowledgements

Thanks are given to the following for the photographs and illustrations used as follows: John Mason for those on pages *ii, iv, vi, viii, ix, xi, xii*, 2, 4, 8, 9, 10 (Nick Drake's grave), 15, 16, 17, 20, 21 (bottom), 22, 24 (top right and bottom), 25, 26, 28 (bottom), 31, 33, 34, 35, 36, 37, 40-41 (hop bines), 46-47 (pylons), 48, 50, 54, 55 (bottom), 58, 60, 62, 63, 64, 65, 66, 67, 68, 75, 76, 77, 78, 80, 81, 82, 83, 84, 85, 86 (top), 87, 88, 92, 93, 94, 95, 96, 98 (bottom), 99, 101, 102, 103, 104, 105, 106, 107, 108, 109, 110, 111, 112 (top), 113, 114, 115, 116, 117, 119, 120, 121, 122, 123, 129, 132 and those on the front and rear cover (top); Logaston Press for those on pages *i, iii*, 1, 3, 7, 19, 21 (top), 23, 27, 28 (top), 29, 30, 32, 38, 39, 42, 44, 45, 46-47 (Coughton valley), 49, 51, 52, 55 (top), 56, 69, 70, 71, 72, 74, 89, 90, 91 (top left), 98 (top), 112 (bottom), 126, 127 and rear cover (bottom); Ken Hutchinson for the maps on pages *xiv* and 19; Andy Stevenson for that on page 6; Cally for that of Nick Drake on page 10; Phil Rickman for that on page 13; Lawrence Hurley for the carving in All Saints on page 24; Tony Williams courtesy of Maureen Beauchamp and the Derek Foxton Collection for the hop-pickers on pages 40-41; Katherina Garratt-Adams for that on page 59; Watkins and Thomas Estate Agents for that on page 73; John Bullough for that top right on page 91; and Bev Craven for the reworking of the image of John Dee on page 128.

A lot of people are due thanks for help putting together the Merrily Watkins stories, and most are credited in various novels. Ced Jackson and Richard Bartholomew, of the British Society of Dowsers, provided extra information for this book, along with various deliverance consultants and ministers, some named, some preferring not to be. Thanks, finally, to Andy & Karen Johnson of Logaston Press for the extra pictures, classy page layouts ... and the determination to get it right.

Corbels at Kilpeck Church

Preface

This book is a result of all the letters and emails which come in daily from readers who say how *real* the Merrily Watkins series feels.

I can't claim too much of the credit for that. As John Mason's pictures demonstrate, virtually all the locations are real, even if some smaller communities are protected by fictional names. And so is much of the background: actual history, legend, folklore and customs, overlaid by recent and current issues.

Essentially, this is a guide to some of the more mysterious elements along the mid and southern Welsh Border. Researching the novels takes me into some areas which seem never to have been fully explored before — certainly not in fiction. You might also find material here which has never appeared in a guide book either. What happens ... putting together a novel, you find yourself drawing together disparate threads, and then, suddenly, you're looking at a whole new tapestry.

As you can imagine, it's quite difficult to make a book like this work without giving away key elements of the fictional plots, but I've tried not to reveal details which might spoil anything for new readers of the novels. To avoid any of those *look away now* moments, information is, just occasionally, incomplete ... although, where possible, other sources are indicated for readers who want to know more.

But, even if you haven't read any of the novels and don't intend to, this book will give you different perspectives on Herefordshire and neighbouring parts of Shropshire, Radnorshire and the Forest of Dean ... areas either side of the Welsh Border which, even when you think you know them, will gradually disclose whole layers of mystery. The Select Bibliography opens up further avenues of exploration.

Phil Rickman

Introduction

A Border Thing

Wern Derys

Borders. For as long as I can remember I've been drawn to them, this one in particular. Borders are risky places, where the unexpected happens. As a kid in Lancashire, an hour or so's drive from Wales, I used to fantasize about what it would be like living on the border. *Right* on the border. One foot in England, one foot in Wales — how would that *feel*?

That was before I'd learned of the very real mystique around borders, the suggestion that a geographical frontier might also be the division between different states of mind, different ways of thinking ... even (careful, now ...) different levels of existence.

Anyway, for most of my adult life, I've lived very close either to the Welsh border or the English border, depending on your standpoint, passing almost daily between the two nations, in an area which is superficially serene but still smouldering with history and clouded with folklore. And now I'm writing novels exploring its textures: a series of novels which seem to have created their own fictional genre: mysteries with more than one layer of mystery.

Mysteries — or so I like to think — in the original sense. The Merrily novels are a combination of the crime thriller and the possibilities of *something else*. Even today, surprisingly few people, locals or incomers, scorn belief in the paranormal. They'll smile sometimes, but they won't scoff.

The series is centred on Herefordshire, extending into Radnor Forest, the hills of Shropshire and Monmouthshire, the Black Mountains and the Malverns. The history and legends of each location tend to invade the stories, along with current issues, and in the end I'm always surprised at how little needs to be made up.

This is a fringe area, in many ways neither England nor Wales, always thinly populated and thus largely ignored by national and regional media. It's always had secrets and usually been able to keep them. The Welsh leader, Owain Glyndwr was last heard of not in the mountains of north Wales but in the Golden Valley of Herefordshire. Salman Rushdie, under Islamic death-sentence, was successfully hidden near Brecon. It's even been rumoured that Lord Lucan, on the run after the murder of his children's nanny, found temporary shelter on the edge of Offa's Dyke before leaving the country.

Less furtively, there was Arthur Conan Doyle tracking the Hound of the Baskervilles, Edward Elgar on his bike, Alfred Watkins sighting ancient tracks between standing stones and steeples.

Today, rock stars and royals find sanctuary here. That famous face you think you saw in Leominster or somewhere ... well, it probably was. This is a safe haven for the famous and the notorious — nobody gets too excited. As my friend Gomer Parry once said, 'En't a problem for us, boy. Long as they don't get too cosy with the sheep.'

Gomer Parry. In many ways, this man *is* the Border. Old but ageless, built like a thorn tree on a hillside facing the west wind, Gomer has hair like a battered lavatory brush, wears thick glasses, smokes roll-ups. Raised in upland, subsistence farming, Gomer decided — long before it became a Government buzz-word — that it was time to diversify.

So he went into Plant Hire. Bought himself a secondhand JCB with which to dig field drains and soakaways for septic tanks. It gave him a certain status, the freedom of the countryside and the ability to crush lesser vehicles with one swing of the bucket. Also a good living because, as he often points out, fields is always gonner need draining and if your soakaway don't soak away you're in deep ... trouble.

Gomer was born in old Radnorshire, at the time the least-known and least-populated county in southern Britain. When my wife, Carol and I were working there as journalists we encountered him — memorably

Looking towards Radnor Forest from Old Radnor

— several times. He's an independent man who observes the natural laws of the countryside and the rules of Plant Hire — digger chivalry. Most of the time he hates the council, the Government and particularly the shiny-arsed townies who run DEFRA (young Jane Watkins says it stands for Destroying Every Farm-reared Animal — Gomer likes that).

It took me a while to get to know Gomer, and it was a few years before I felt qualified to write about him, having observed his basic rule for survival on the Border: keep real quiet till you knows the score.

Surprising how many people get that one wrong and wind up face-down in the old slurry pit.

The first Merrily Watkins novel, *The Wine of Angels*, was to have been a Gomer Parry novel until a pivotal aspect of the plot made it necessary for the village of Ledwardine to have a woman vicar.

After which, Merrily, in her insecure, self-effacing, less-than-confident way, took over.

In the next novel, *Midwinter of the Spirit*, she was appointed diocesan exorcist for Hereford and became a series. Now, if you Google exorcism/Hereford in the hope of finding someone to help you over some domestic intrusion you can't rationally explain, I'm afraid you're likely to be directed, at some stage, to Merrily Watkins.

She's embarrassed, of course. Merrily isn't into fame or the cult-of-personality. This wasn't at all what she had in mind when she arrived in the village of Ledwardine as a thirty-something widow with a slightly resentful teenage daughter, Jane, who at first didn't want to be here and definitely didn't want her mum to be a vicar, not least because her own spiritual leanings were distinctly pagan.

To be honest, I never imagined anyone could write a whole series of fairly dark crime novels from the point of view of a country vicar, female or male. I had no idea, back then, that she was going to turn, quite rapidly, into the best idea I'd ever had.

Bredwardine Bridge across the Wye

Map of the area

1   Old Cider

Twisty old devil.
Looked as if it held a grudge in every scabby branch, and
it wouldn't give you any fruit, on principle. Because, left to
rot, apple trees ...
                           ... they grows resentful.
Merrily's grandad had told her that once, when she was a little
girl. Frightening her ...

The Wine of Angels

Like most vicars, Merrily is from Off. She has ancestry in the area, but did her training in Liverpool. She's a thirty-something widow with a teenage daughter. She smokes. When she drops something on her foot she doesn't say, 'Oh, bother'. And, no, she *doesn't* look like Dawn French.

Bringing in a stranger is always a useful device for a novelist. After all, most of the readers are also going to be from Off, so viewing an area through the eyes of an outsider lets you dwell on its eccentricities, highlighting both appealing blemishes and sinister stains which locals might no longer notice.

The village of Ledwardine is the missing location on the Herefordshire Black and White Trail. Think timber-framing and white plaster. Think Pembridge, Weobley, Dilwyn, Eardisland; Ledwardine has bits of all of them. It used to be a working village, sustained by farming and the cider industry, but its current prosperity is largely a result of its olde worlde appeal. Here's what it says on a notorious website sponsored by estate agents keen to persuade wealthy folk from Off to move in.

Unicorn House, Weobley

LEDWARDINE

Once known as The Village in the Orchard, this community may have begun as simply that. The old centre of the village is still partly enclosed by the remains of an apple orchard dating back at least to medieval times, as do some of its black and white timber-framed houses. Earlier settlement is suggested by recent archaeological discoveries at the foot of Cole Hill, whose Iron Age fortifications are a reminder of a turbulent past. Today, Ledwardine ('Jewel of The New Cotswolds' – *Daily Telegraph*) is serene and inviting. The cobbled village square, with its small, open market-hall supported by oak pillars, is enlivened by a variety of retail outlets, including a bookshop, gallery and delicatessen, as well as the 15th-century Black Swan Inn, noted for its fine food.

FACILITIES: the village, although largely self-sufficient, is a mere ten minute drive from the nearest town of Leominster and no more than twenty-five minutes from the progressive cathedral city of Hereford, now undergoing extensive commercial renewal. Several highly reputable private schools are within easy reach.

LEDWARDINE STAR-RATING **** *and rising!*

WE SAY: *buy now*, while prices are competitive and this area is still relatively obscure.

Pembridge

Clockwise from above: Weobley Church; The Throne, Weobley; New Inn, Pembridge; Pembridge; Church Tower, Pembridge

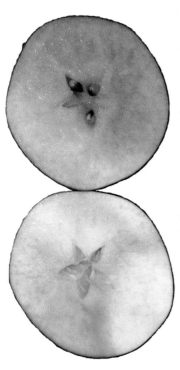

Note the orchard, central to *The Wine of Angels* and, nine books later, *To Dream of the Dead*. Like many apparently-innocuous features of the border, it's more than it seems. When Merrily arrives in Ledwardine, as priest-in-charge, there's blood on the apple trees and more trouble to come. Incomers to Ledwardine are promoting a summer festival designed to raise the village's prominence on the tourist map and revive the traditional local cider. Meanwhile, the truth is about to be uncovered about a 17th-century vicar accused of witchcraft. Then a teenage girl goes missing — and not the first.

This book is full of apples. Apples and cider, apples and murder, apples and the unseen. For example, as the old folklorist Lucy Devenish explains to Jane Watkins, if you cut an apple crossways — that is, not through the stalk — you'll find ...

'There.' She held out a half in the palm of each hand. 'What do you see?'

Jane leaned over the counter. The green-white pulp was veined with thin green lines and dots which made a kind of wheel.

'Count the spokes,' Lucy said.

'Five.'

'It makes a five-pointed star, you see? Inside a circle. A pentagram ... a very ancient symbol of purification and protection. And there's one at the heart of every apple. That says something, doesn't it?'

Lucy Devenish runs a small, crowded shop called Ledwardine Lore, which provides exactly what it says on the sign. Lucy knows more than anybody about the village's secrets, many of which relate to ...

Cider

Which, in Herefordshire, goes back, almost certainly, to pre-Roman times, although the Romans apparently preferred perry (the equivalent, made from pears). It's been in and out of fashion ever since, always popular with farmworkers, occasionally favoured by the gentry, especially in the 18th century. There are still said to be nearly ten thousand acres of cider orchard in the county. Several independent cider companies are still based there, while Hereford's best-known cider firm, Bulmers, has changed hands twice recently, with owners from Off replaced by owners from seriously Off. You can find out how the wine of angels was originally made in the cider museum by the side of Sainsbury's. A shadowy place with the dense musky atmosphere I wanted the novel to carry.

I've always enjoyed discovering a weird underside to familiar items: the poisoned apple, the worm in the apple, so it was good to find someone of a similar mind, even if long dead. Much of the folklore in this novel and several of the others was plucked from the pages of an invaluable book by

Ella Mary Leather

Published in 1912, Mrs Leather's *The Folklore of Herefordshire* may be the best collection of local legends and traditions ever published in Britain. At least, I've never found one more detailed. This inquisitive Victorian lady (born 1874) hung out with gypsies and old farmworkers and burrowed deep into the red border soil to uncover half-buried pagan roots, customs, traditions, superstitions, folk tales, folk song ...

Ella Mary Leather

the rhythm and pulse of the Border.

'No record in cold print can give the reader an idea of the pleasure experienced in collecting the elusive material we call folk lore from the living brains of men and women of whose lives it has formed an integral part,' she writes in her preface, after relating how it all began with Martha B—

> ... a tiny, dark-haired, olive skinned woman who, when I first remembered her, gathered apples in a Herefordshire orchard ... Martha smoked a little clay pipe, apologetically 'by doctor's orders'; her greeting was always 'Good day, missie, God bless you'; I learned that this formula was an infallible protection against witchcraft and the evil eye. It was Martha who could tell how the house which once stood in the wood had been pulled down because it was so badly haunted; she herself saw ghosts and could point out the very spots where they appeared to her.

Mrs Leather was from Weobley, a place very close to Ledwardine. If she'd been born 50 years later, she would almost certainly have been Lucy Devenish's best friend.

The only book to pick up Mrs Leather's trail in recent years is Roy Palmer's *Herefordshire Folklore*, part of his valuable and timely series, which also deals with Radnorshire, Shropshire, Monmouthshire and Worcestershire. Arguably, still the most mysterious area of southern Britain.

On the advice of Ella Mary, I called the original Ledwardine cider apple the *Pharisees Red* — the *pharisees* a corruption of *farises*, an archaic local word for fairies, whose tiny lights, according to legend, may be seen in the Ledwardine orchard, along with bits of old Edgar Powell, who blows his head off with a 12-bore shotgun during an attempted revival of

Wassailing

This is a custom usually carried out on Twelfth Night in an attempt to ensure a good crop of apples the following autumn. It's been revived in Herefordshire over the past twenty years, with wassails in Much

Marcle in the east and Eardisley in the west. In can involve pouring cider over the roots of an apple tree or, as in *The Wine of Angels*, firing shotguns through the branches after an appropriately encouraging chant.

The Twelfth Night ceremonies may have begun with the lighting of fires in wheat fields to encourage healthy crops. The lighting up of the darkest time of the year. The pagan origins are clear. Mrs Leather also describes a ritual I just had to borrow, which seems to get inside the earth itself.

> The men stand in a ring around the fire and 'holloa auld cider'. They sing on one very deep note, very slowly, holding each syllable as long as possible, 'Auld—Ci—der.' The 'der' becomes a sort of growl at the end and is an octave below the first two notes; it has a weird dirge-like effect.

The title of this novel comes from the line 'Tears are the wine of angels, the best ... to quench the devil's fires' attributed to a 17th-century Herefordshire poet and mystic whose work is often quoted in the book to echo certain themes.

Thomas Traherne (1637-1674)

The son of a Hereford shoemaker, Traherne became Rector of Credenhill several centuries before the SAS moved in. Lucy Devenish was not the only person to have detected elements of paganism or at least pantheism in his poetry.

Essentially, Traherne was a pre-hippy advocate of happiness ... *felicity*. He knew and loved the countryside in all its jewelled moods. His philosophy was, *God gave it to you — enjoy*. In fact, he suggested, *not* enjoying it was an insult to creation, and his lines,

You never enjoy the world aright
Till the sea itself floweth in your veins
Till you are clothed in the heavens
And crowned with the stars

Credenhill Church

were memorably set to music, at the zenith of psychedelia, by Mike Heron of The Incredible String Band, who clearly held similar views.

In *The Wine of Angels*, Lucy Devenish introduces Traherne's poems to Lol Robinson, a songwriter and musician who gets closer, with almost every book, to Merrily Watkins. Lol's career in folk-rock, with the band Hazey Jane, was cut short in difficult circumstances. He finds himself relating increasingly to the artist who influenced his earliest songs and provided the band with its name:

This page & opposite: Stained glass in Hereford Cathedral by Tom Denny inspired by Thomas Traherne

Nick Drake (1948-1974)

Lol is one of the many contemporary singer-songwriters influenced to the point of minor obsession by someone far more famous now than he ever was in his brief lifetime. In a way, Lol, though more than twenty years younger, is what Nick Drake might have become if he'd survived.

Nick's songs, like *Way to Blue*, *Hazey Jane II*, *River Man*, *From the Morning*, convey a unique sense of wistful, pastoral Englishness. The problem at the time of their release was that there were just so many ground-breaking albums around that it was easy for something this subtle and restrained to fall through the cracks.

Nick Drake

The albums had poor sales. It didn't help that Nick himself was becoming increasingly withdrawn and had problems facing an audience. Someone who went to one of his very rare concerts told me he'd physically half-turn himself away from the crowd.

Eventually, it became clear that Nick was becoming mentally ill. He died at his parents' home in Tanworth-in-Arden, Warwickshire, from an overdose of anti-depressants which may or may not have been accidental. You can hear the chill of despair in his later songs, in the elemental menace of *Pink Moon* and the raw bleakness of *Black Eyed Dog*.

It wasn't until the mid-1990s that Nick's three albums, *Five Leaves Left*, *Bryter Layter* and *Pink Moon*, took off, artists including Paul Weller and Beth Orton having identified him as a major influence. In 2007, after many bootlegs, his early home-recordings, which included his mother Molly's own surprisingly effective songs, were finally released as the album *Family Tree*, with sleeve-notes (and a duet on the sadly prophetic cover of *All My Trials, Soon Be Over*) by his sister, the actress Gabrielle Drake.

Around the time of *Family Tree*, I finally went to Tanworth-in-Arden. As did Lol Robinson, in the ninth novel, *The Fabric of Sin*.

Nick shares with his parents, Molly and Rodney, a modest stone under an oak tree in the raised churchyard at Tanworth. It's a lovely spot which will always, for me, carry a soundtrack of *From the Morning*, the soft, summery final song on the final album. For Lol, inevitably, it was more complicated and, with the help of Gabrielle Drake and Cally, who handles Nick's business affairs, we were able to catch the moment on the abridged audio book of *Fabsin*. Lol's own collections, 'Songs from Lucy's Cottage' and 'A Message from the Morning' (music and lyrics by Allan Watson and Phil Rickman), are available as CDs — details on the website www. philrickman.co.uk.

Nick Drake's grave

Meanwhile, back in *The Wine of Angels*, Merrily is faced with a series of inexplicable and possibly paranormal events in and around the 17th-century crookedly timber-framed vicarage where she and Jane live. She tries to elicit some advice from her employers on how to deal with them, only to find that the Church of England tends to consider the idea of psychic phenomena slightly embarrassing. Slowly, Merrily finds out who her friends are: Lucy Devenish, the folklorist, Lol Robinson, the songwriter, and Gomer Parry who, in semi-retirement from Plant Hire, digs the graves and looks after the churchyard.

It isn't until the second book, *Midwinter of the Spirit*, that Merrily becomes aware of the Deliverance ministry, the Church's secret service.

2   Something a bit dark

After *Wine* I couldn't bring myself to dump Merrily. Or Jane. Particularly Jane. But I definitely didn't want to write a series of what are known in the USA as 'clerical mysteries' in which persons of the cloth implausibly investigate cosy murders. If Merrily was to survive, she had to be authentically employed in some area of the job which might realistically involve her with criminal behaviour and the underside of spirituality.

The answer appeared to lie in Deliverance. Or, as it was previously known, exorcism — the name having been changed, in the Anglican church, as a result of a horrifyingly frenzied murder.

In 1974, just a year after shocking scenes of demonic possession in the film *The Exorcist* had led to medical alerts in cinemas all over Britain, a 31-year-old unemployed handyman called Michael Taylor, from Ossett, near Barnsley, went to a local minister, claiming to be possessed by devils. Two priests subsequently embarked on an all-night exorcism, after which they told him they'd cast out an estimated forty demons.

Taylor then went home and savagely killed his wife, tearing out her eyes and her tongue.

Within the Church of England, this had repercussions at the highest level. The Archbishop of Canterbury at the time, Donald Coggan, said, 'We must get this business out of the mumbo-jumbo of magic. I think there are many cases where the more rash exorcists have bypassed the work of psychiatrists.'

New rules and new guidelines for exorcists were introduced — followed, twelve years later, by the official casting-out of the term exorcism. Henceforth, each diocese would have a Deliverance adviser, whose own advisers should include a psychiatrist. The new watchword was caution, and it still is.

A former deliverance minister in Herefordshire said, 'I always remember my predecessor saying to me, "This is a mucky world and you come across mucky things. It's not a very nice job. You get a sense of something a bit dark." He was right. You do find strange circumstances and disturbed people. You can actually feel the hairs going up on the back of your neck even while you're looking for the rational explanations.'

Because of increasing demand and the need, these days, always to cover your back, one deliverance minister per diocese is often seen as insufficient. Now it tends to be a team, whose main function is to offer advice and support to local priests faced with aspects of the unexplained in their parishes.

In a big diocese there could be twelve people involved, including psychiatrists. Which means there are now more trained exorcists working in the UK than at any time in the history of the Church ... and this in a so-called secular age.

'We are, in a way, getting more medieval with every year that passes,' says Canon Michael Wadsworth, for some years a member of a deliverance team based at Ely in the Cambridgeshire Fens. 'There's a sense in which secular men and woman tend to believe a lot more — things their grandparents would have thought rubbish. And the difference now is that people want to do something about it.'

I've learned a lot about the procedures and the pitfalls of exorcism in the ten years since the Merrily Watkins series began. From the start, I wanted the stories to be absolutely authentic. No gratuitous horror, no hint of fantasy ... and a central character who is flawed, paranoid and doesn't always get it right.

At first, the clergy I approached for background information were understandably suspicious. Then, after the second novel, a deliverance minister — someone I didn't, at the time, know — emailed to say he thought the low-key approach and the balance between the real and the imagined were 'exactly right'. As other approving emails filtered through from what's regarded as the coal-face of Christianity, I learned a lot ... and realised that Merrily, with her nicotine habit, her uncertainty and her occasional lapses into language not found in prayer books, wasn't exactly the maverick I'd initially had in mind. Closer, in fact, to the norm.

Deliverance is the Church's secret service, often regarded with suspicion within the C of E, in much the same way as the police mistrust the spooks of Special Branch. Some image-conscious senior clerics see it as a potentially dangerous throwback to the days of the Witchfinder General.

Which may be why deliverance ministers are usually hand-picked by their bishops. Like Merrily, they are often reluctant to take on a role which involves dealing with both human delusion and — even worse — the possibility that some of it *isn't* delusion.

The priests who actually volunteer for deliverance work, in the hope of a hand-to-hand scrap with the powers of evil, are the ones considered least suitable for the job. What the Church is looking for, it seems, is a quality of restraint. And, when you need to separate the real from the imagined, a touch of scepticism is also helpful.

'Someone who says "I need to be exorcized" is usually someone looking for an easy answer,' one exorcist told me, and someone who should be handled with protective gloves. But if even alleged spiritual invasion of a person is rare, property is more vulnerable. It's mainly about ghosts.

The two most commonly reported phenomena encountered by the deliverance ministry are poltergeists and what have become known as 'bereavement apparitions' — sightings, usually by close relatives, of the newly-dead.

It's been estimated that one in four bereaved relatives — husbands and wives, sons and daughters — or even work colleagues will catch occasional glimpses of the departed in familiar spots. A deliverance co-ordinator in Herefordshire says it can sometimes become contagious.

'While many will have some hazy experiences of seeing or hearing the person who has died — which will cease — for a few, these continue and become very vivid, especially if the death was unexpected or complicated. Other people close to the bereaved person may come to share these experiences and reinforce the problem of being unable to let go of the dead person.'

This might be treated by an explanatory chat over a cup of tea, and perhaps prayers or, in extreme cases, a Requiem Eucharist — in effect a second funeral service.

But what are we talking about here? Is it an actual ghost or what psychiatrists would call a psychological projection?

The current co-chairman of British exorcism's governing body, the Christian Deliverance Study Group, is the Bishop of Monmouth, Dominic Walker, perhaps Britain's most experienced exorcist.

Bishop Dominic comes across as urbane, laid-back and well practised in the art of understatement. He says he believes that ninety per cent of all apparitions are mental projections, and it takes some prompting to get him to talk about the time he believes he actually stood next to one.

A ghost, that is. A *real* ghost.

A family had moved into a house to find that the upstairs was already occupied by a middle-aged woman with one leg who would appear and then vanish before their eyes. It emerged that a woman had, in fact, committed suicide there not long after having a leg amputated.

Dominic Walker decided to assemble the family for a Requiem Eucharist — a communion service or Anglican mass for the repose of the dead — in the bedroom where the woman had died, using a dressing table as an altar. Contrary to popular belief, ghosts are not actually exorcised in the *get thee hence* sense; the aim is to direct them towards eternal peace.

'And as we were celebrating the mass, she appeared,' the Bishop recalled. 'It wasn't a frightening experience. It just looked as if we'd been joined by someone else, and that person had only one leg. I thought, Either this is *my* psychological projection or I've been set up. It was only at the end of the service that members of the family said to me, Do you know that when you were praying for her she appeared?'

The woman, he says, finally vanished, never to return.

But it isn't always so easy. Sometimes it takes repeated Requiems and aftercare. A woman minister told me of a case where an apparent poltergeist turned into something out of Hitchcock's Psycho — a man attacked in the shower looked down to find blood issuing from a cut in his leg.

Strange, angelic figures appear in a picture I took at Garway

'I told the couple I wanted to say prayers in the house and then blessed water and salt and blessed each room. Which was fine till I reached the landing between the bedroom and bathroom.

'The back of my neck was crawling, and I felt cold but there was no draught, and I realised how hard it was getting to say the prayer I wanted to say. I had to concentrate to get my mouth to make the words. It was like I could hear them in my head, but something was stopping me from forming them.

'And I felt threatened, like something was trying to force me to stop. I was actually quite scared of what would happen. I could feel something surrounding me. I guess it felt like it would attack if it could, but as long as I kept saying the words, it couldn't. But saying the words was so hard.

'With hindsight, I think that there was a fight-back on that landing. I was aware of an anger, rage even. Mostly I just get aware of whatever it is, but no real fight. The house is free of problems now, anyway.'

Canon Michael Wadsworth recalls going with another priest to help a colleague suffering psychic persecution in his own vicarage.

'Ornaments — some quite heavy — were moving, often in the middle of the night. He was distraught — at the end of his tether. There was definitely a malign influence — a troubled spirit.

'We conducted a Requiem Eucharist and opened every window and every door — it was a fine summer's day. While we worked inside the house, he went outside and shouted at the top of his voice, "Do your bloody worst!"'

Apparently, it worked.

What was perhaps Michael Wadsworth's most curious case involved a very old prayer book given as a legacy to his church. It had belonged to a priest and went into general use.

'It was interesting how, in at least two homes belonging to people who attended the church and used that particular prayer book, things started to happen — poltergeist phenomena and voices. I didn't tell people, just ceased to use the prayer book and blessed it, privately. And it stopped.

'I'm probably being whimsical about it, but being in my job makes you like this. I've come away with the lifetime motto: there's no such thing as a gratuitous coincidence. Sometimes it seems as if we're trembling on the brink of the absurd, but religion is like that.'

If all this has made it seem relatively easy — a splash of holy water, a well-timed ritual and, even if there's a struggle, the good guys always win — it's important to point out that it *doesn't* always work. Most deliverance ministers have painful ongoing cases they can't discuss because the victims would be identified.

There are apparent presences which repeated Requiem eucharists have failed to erase. There are cases where parish priests have suffered breakdowns or even quit the ministry. Most deliverance ministers will tell you they've watched objects move or at least felt the intense cold, a cold you experience inside as a kind of frigid void. The borderline between psychiatric illness and what one senior exorcist calls psychic or demonic *oppression* is continually blurred.

In *Midwinter of the Spirit*, a new bishop of Hereford, having heard of Merrily's problems in *The Wine of Angels*, invites her to take on the additional job of deliverance consultant for the diocese.

Consultant is an appropriate word, as the diocesan exorcist is mostly there to advise. If you have a problem, you normally take it to the local vicar or rector who may then refer it to the deliverance minister.

Which is what I did, approaching the then deliverance minister for Hereford to ask him what kind of a job he thought this would be for a woman.

'A very dangerous one,' he said.

3   Midwinter

> Under the window, a fourteenth-century bishop slept on, his marble
> mitre like a nightcap. But the tomb of his saintly predecessor, Thomas
> Cantilupe, was in pieces — stone sections laid out, Merrily thought,
> like a display of postmodern garden ornaments.
>
> *Midwinter of the Spirit*

Midwinter enters the old city of Hereford, its cathedral, its secret history.

The deliverance consultant is appointed by the Bishop, who must approve any major exorcism. To put Merrily right at the heart of things, I gave her an office at the cathedral and a time-share in the Bishop's lay-secretary, Sophie Hill, a smart, elegant, slightly severe woman who 'works for the Cathedral'.

Sophie's office, and Merrily's Hereford deliverance base, is above the gatehouse, overlooking Broad Street and the Cathedral green. Across the road in Gwynne Street, is the home of the former diocesan exorcist, Canon Thomas Dobbs, a man bitterly opposed to the idea of a woman deliverance consultant, pointing out that 'the first exorcist was Jesus Christ'. Dobbs is determined that Merrily should be exposed to deliverance at its most disturbing.

Cathedral gatehouse

As *Midwinter* opens, she's learning about the rules and techniques of exorcism in a remote part of the Brecon Beacons, where the SAS do their training (and where exorcism *is* taught). The course leader and Merrily's spiritual director is the Rev. Huw Owen, blunt, cynical but far from sceptical. The danger of being a woman exorcist? Huw doesn't dress it up.

... headlights floated down the valley, a long way away. She thought of Jane back home in Ledwardine and felt isolated, cut off. A night breeze razored down from crags she could no longer see.

'Listen,' Huw said, 'the ordination of women is indisputably the most titillating development in the Church since the Reformation. They'll follow you home, they'll breathe into your phone at night, break into your vestry and tamper with your gear. Crouch in the back pews and masturbate through your sermons ... prime target for every psychotic grinder of the dark satanic mills that ever sacrificed a chicken ...'

Merrily's first assignment takes her to the old Hereford General Hospital, once the city's lunatic asylum, where she encounters a patient who makes even seasoned nurses nervous. This incident is based almost entirely on a story I was told by a local former nursing sister.

Fairly soon, a body is recovered from the River Wye near Victoria Bridge, not far from the old hospital and the story switches to Dinedor Hill and the Cathedral and the ancient church of St Cosmas and St Damian, by way of the Dinedor ley and the legacy of

Gwynne Street, Hereford

16

Above: Hereford Cathedral and Bishops Palace across the Wye; Below: Victoria suspension bridge, Hereford

Alfred Watkins

You won't find an official monument to Alfred Watkins in Hereford — an almost criminal omission. There used to be a short footpath by the side of Tesco called Watkins Way, but even that disappeared. All that remains is the plaque on his former house near the Cathedral.

Watkins was a county councillor, a magistrate, a brewer, a pioneer photographer, an archaeologist and, for thousands of people all over the world, the most important Herefordian in history. For this was the man who discovered leys.

OK, *I* don't know whether or not leys exist. All I know is that the *idea* of them changed the way I look at a landscape, gave me a feel for patterns of hills and meadows, mounds and churches that I never had before. Or maybe, subliminally, I did. Maybe we all do; whatever, Alfred Watkins' contribution to our perception of Britain is unique.

A ley is a — usually invisible — line which Watkins believed linked ancient monuments. He worked out that many Bronze Age ritual sites — standing stones, stone circles, burial mounds — had been arranged to follow straight lines across the countryside. As many medieval and pre-medieval churches were built on sites of earlier worship and castle mottes were sometimes formed around burial mounds, they would also sometimes occur on straight lines. Watkins presented his theories to the Woolhope Naturalists' Field Club which, of course, still exists, and published them in *Early British Trackways* and his most celebrated work, *The Old Straight Track*, a book which continues to change lives.

Alfred Watkins' original research was conducted on maps and on foot. If you stand on the edge of the Iron Age camp on Dinedor Hill and look across the city you can actually see one of his most famous leys. Stand where you can align the Cathedral tower with the spire of All Saints and you're on it.

What does this mean?

Watkins was a little cagey about it. He rarely went further than the suggestion that leys were ancient trackways, possible trading routes. But when you read between the lines of *The Old Straight Track* it's clear that he was sensing a greater mystery.

It was left to a succession of later writers to develop the more seductive theories. The occultist Dion Fortune was the first to suggest, in her novel *The Goatfoot God*, that Watkins' leys might be channels of psychic energy, a theory adopted by dowsers, who began to track the lines with rods and pendulums, and developed by John Michell in his seminal book, *The View over Atlantis*.

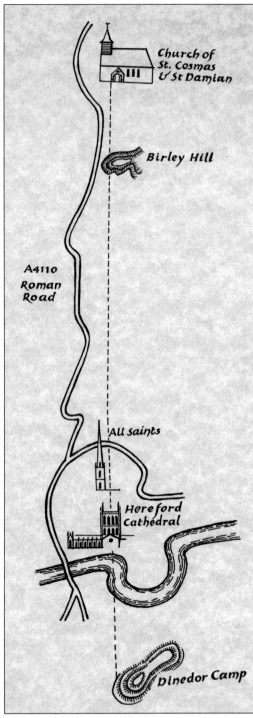

Above: Sketch map of the ley line running
between Dinedor Camp and the church
of Saints Cosmas and Damian
Top left: Alfred Watkins' house, Hereford
Lower left: Church Street, Hereford

The latest theory, promoted by the writer Paul Devereux and others, is that leys were 'spirit roads', routes along which the dead were believed to walk and where tribal shamans sought communication with them. Supporting evidence for this includes the tradition of 'coffin paths' — established routes by which the dead were taken into country churches, seen as memories of leys — and, of course, the tendency for ghost sightings to be reported on leys.

The narrow Church Street, or Capuchin Way, which links Hereford Cathedral with High Town follows one of Watkins' leys. This is where Merrily's friend, Lol Robinson lives in *Midwinter of the Spirit*.

But the Dinedor ley, passing through the centre of the city and the cathedral itself, is central to the plot ... and one of the few it's possible to see almost from beginning to end.

Dinedor Hill

... is often said to be Hereford's mother hill. This may be where the city began, as an Iron Age camp, the ramparts of which can still be seen in the shade of mature trees at the top of the hill.

Although the name Dinedor comes from the ancient British or Welsh *dyn*, meaning fort, the earthworks on the hill suggest a community rather than a military base, and the idea of an earlier ritual site on the hill has been strengthened by the recent discovery of the Dinedor Serpent or Rotherwas Ribbon, of which more later.

If we follow the line to Hereford Cathedral we encounter the shrine of

Dinedor Hill

Dinedor Hillfort and summit

This shrine was probably second only to Thomas Becket's in Canterbury Cathedral as a centre of healing. Candles may still be lit at the refurbished tomb in the north transept.

Cantilupe Shrine, Hereford Cathedral

Born around 1218, Tommy Canty, as he's affectionately known to Merrily's spiritual director, Huw Owen, was the most celebrated medieval bishop of Hereford, a man revered in his lifetime who, it was said, could bring little birds to the window when he celebrated mass. An experienced lawyer, he was appointed Bishop of Hereford in 1275, in the reign of Edward I. In a dispute with the Archbishop of Canterbury, Thomas was excommunicated, went to Rome to appeal to the Pope and died of a fever. His body was boiled to remove the flesh and his bones brought back to Hereford, where they were entombed, originally in the Lady Chapel before a new shrine was built in the north transept in 1287.

By this time, miracles were being reported, beginning with the calming of a Hereford ironmonger's wife who, possibly because of a drink problem, attacked her husband, bit her mother and harangued God and the neighbours. She claimed to have a vision of 'Saint' Thomas, although he wouldn't be canonised until 1320.

About 500 miraculous cures were claimed over the next twenty-five years, with pilgrims being carried into the cathedral on stretchers and walking out. People too ill to be carried to the Cathedral were measured in string which was then used as the wick of a candle dedicated to St Thomas. Animals, too, were cured.

Around the time *Midwinter* was taking shape, the tomb was dismantled for cleaning, repair and refurbishment, for the first time since 1860 when, I was told, something very disturbing was found inside. Not this time, however.

As far as I know.

All Saints Church, Hereford

... is the next point on the ley.

With its flourishing café, All Saints on a weekday has a real feel of what you imagine a church would have been like in medieval times, the vibrant centre of a community. It also has a ghost who likes to sit near

All Saints Church, Hereford

23

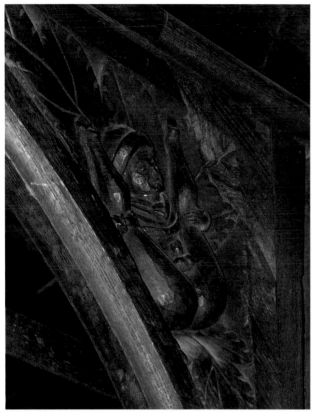

Carving at All Saints Church, Hereford   *Sheelagh-na-gig, Kilpeck Church*

the organ. And, talking of organs, in the café area upstairs there's a carving which suggests a male sheelagh-na-gig ... a rampant little figure linked to fertility.

De Bere tomb and Church of St Cosmas and St Damian, Stretford

The healing theme of the Dinedor ley is picked up again at its final point.

The Church of St Cosmas and St Damian

This mysterious little double-naved church in the hamlet of Stretford, near Dilwyn, is dedicated to two 4th-century saints linked with physicians and surgeons and, although made redundant in 1969, was used until quite recently for an annual thanksgiving service for doctors and nurses.

A healing well is said to have disappeared from the church precincts, although many people still regard it as a centre of healing, and ley-hunters have pointed to some old stones in the raised churchyard as evidence of pagan worship. However, when we visited the church in March 2007 for a TV programme which, in the end, was never made, archaeologist Jodie Lewis suggested the stones might actually be the remains of the holy well.

St Cosmas and St Damian has been maintained by the Churches Conservation Trust, remains consecrated, and occasional services are still held there ...

Church of St Cosmas and St Damian, Stretford

... unlike some churches along the Border which have fallen into disuse and, in a few cases, into ruins. Reverting, some would say, to their ancient origins as circles of stone ...

Church of St Cosmas and St Damian, Stretford

4   Witchlights

Curtains of cold, red light hung from the heavens into the
roofless nave. When Robin emerged from the tower, she took
his cold hand in her even colder ones. The church was
mournful around her.

A Crown of Lights

Now it's coming up to Candlemas, or Imbolc, the old Celtic festival of the first light, celebrated in early
February, and we slip into mid-Wales, directly into the path of ...

The Dragon

There are five medieval churches in and around Radnor Forest, all dedicated to St Michael, the archangel
responsible for dealing with dragons.

We lived in Radnor for over fifteen years, and although I never actually saw a dragon I did once photograph what ghost-hunters like to call 'an orb' and ufologists like to call, um, a UFO, over Castell Crugeryr,
a very prominent castle mound off an elbow of road near Fforest Inn.

Castell Crugeryr in snow

Tomen Castle on the lower slopes of Radnor Forest

The Four Stones

Discoed

It's an odd place, Radnor Forest. Not a forest in the accepted sense, as it actually has comparatively few trees. Forest, traditionally, was just a term for a hunting ground. This is an area of wild green hills, and the smallest hills are the castle mounds, several — Castell Crugeryr, Tomen Castle, New Radnor Castle, Hundred House Mount — visible from the country lanes known as the A44 and A481 which slither across it.

The Forest also has some nicely-obscure prehistoric stones — notably the Four Stones near Kinnerton, which appear in the third Merrily novel, *A Crown of Lights*.

Behind a hedge, this is a safe, almost cosy site from which to contemplate the quarry-savaged skyline and the lofty Old Radnor church to the west.

Old Radnor, dominant though it appears, is not one of the five St Michael churches which form a slightly squashed pentagram across the hills, extending from Cefnllys — lovely spot — near Llandrindod Wells, up to Llanfihangel Rhydithon, down to Llanfihangel-nant-Melan, Cascob and finally Discoed with its venerable yew tree, close to the English border.

A stretch of hillside near Llandegley, in the Forest, is still known as The Dragon's Back, and a former clergyman at Llanfihangel Rhydithon wrote,

> I often spoke to an old man who lived up on the slopes of the Forest and maintained that though he had never seen it he had heard it breathing. Was it because of the dragon that our Christian ancestors ringed it around with St Michael churches ...?

Several sources suggest that Radnor Forest was particularly vulnerable to the forces of darkness and required protection at the highest level. One legend warns that if any of the churches is allowed to close, the evil will return.

But what was meant by evil?

Is the dragon simply a symbol of the ancient pagan religions represented by the standing stones, circles and mounds all over Radnor Forest? (As *A Crown of Lights* was being written, archaeologists were documenting the discovery of a massive henge in the Radnor Valley, not far from the location of the novel's one invented village, Old Hindwell.) Or was there believed to be a real and active evil which could be repelled only be a combination of old and new religion?

Llandegley Rocks — The Dragon's Back

The Charms

The idea for *A Crown of Lights* began to ferment when a member of an old Radnorshire family, Glyn Morgan, sent me a copy of a charm found in a farmhouse in north Radnorshire invoking holy names to protect the farmer, his horses, cows, sheep, pigs and poultry from molestation, witches' spells and the power of Satan.

Its mixture of Christianity and paganism was remarkably similar to a well-known exorcism which you can still see on a wall of the most remote of St Michael churches at Cascob. Dating back to round 1700, it's known as the Abracadabra Charm because of its traditional use of a magic word since devalued by genera-tions of stage magicians.

A B R A C A D A B R A
A B R A C A D A B
A B R A C A D
A B R A C
A B R
A

In the name of the Father, son and the Holy Ghost Amen x x x and in the name of the Lord Jesus Christ I will deliver Elizabeth Loyd from all witchcraft and from all Evil spirites & from all evil men or Women or Wizardes or hardness of hart Amen x x x

Cascob Church

The site of Ednol Church; (above) the ruins of Llanwarne (opposite)

So was there, in Radnor Forest, a hybrid religion, a form of semi-pagan hedge-Christianity, and what remains of it today?

In *A Crown of Lights*, a pagan couple move into a farmhouse and are presented by 'the local people' with a copy of a similar protective charm, before becoming the target of what is effectively a witch hunt led by a fundamentalist Anglican priest with a few secrets of his own.

The farmhouse happens to have, on its land, a ruined church, which forms part of the protective pentagram of St Michael churches. To avoid ruining the reputation of an existing ruined church, I had to invent one. However there is one in Radnor Forest, Ednol, of which rather less remains than the church at Old Hindwell. There are also a couple of ruins in Herefordshire which fit the image. The first is at Llanwarne, a few miles from Ross-on-Wye. And the other — which also serves as an introduction to the Frome Valley, location of the next chapter — illustrates another aspect of exorcism.

Avenbury Church

The remains of St Mary's, Avenbury, lie in a shallow grave of tangled woodland, enclosed by tall trees, embalmed by creepers. Mentioned in the Domesday Book of 1086, the church was decommissioned by the diocese in 1946 ... and if you're alone here at dusk, just be grateful for the silence.

The ghost stories have been circulating for at least fifty years. It's said that a church organ sometimes moans at close of day. That bells peal in the roofless tower. That a company of cowled monks still sings in the opened shell of the nave.

'No, I don't particularly like the place,' the Rev. Graham Sykes says carefully. 'It makes me feel uneasy.'

Graham, vicar of Bromyard in East Herefordshire, is responsible for the former parish of Avenbury where this church was left to rot. It might be a thousand years old, but it was never an architectural treasure. Another local vicar has visited it just once and has no plans to return.

'It's a horrible place. It just *feels* horrible. I've never been anywhere before where I've felt so much ... badness.'

But it's not the ghostly monks that offend the local clergy, or the spooky soundtrack. It's the fact that St Mary's still seems to be a place of worship.

This page and opposite: Avenbury Church

The wrong kind, of course. Like many medieval churches, it's believed to occupy a place of pre-Christian sanctity, and its absentee owner actually erected a sign identifying it as an 'ancient pagan site'. So now, as its stonework crumbles, St Mary's has become fully available, day and night, for ... well, for anything you fancy, basically.

Amongst the rubble below the tower's last remaining rafter, I found signs of a recent fire and the remains of candles burned on the broken graves of local families. The suspicion, naturally, is of black magic rites or at least occult games involving teenagers attracted by the church's sinister reputation and its isolation.

'I do think places are affected by the things that happen in them,' Graham Sykes says. 'I think kids have been going out there, maybe at night, for a laugh.'

But when the laughter dies and they go home alone, perhaps wondering what they might have disturbed ... that's often when the problems begin.

As recently as last year, a small outbreak of apparent poltergeist phenomena was reported at homes in the area — moving objects, footsteps heard overhead, cold spots. Several of these cases were said to have involved families known to be fascinated by the ruins of St Mary's Church. The talk was of ouija-board experiments — attempts to contact the unquiet dead of Avenbury.

As the building isn't theirs any more, there's nothing the Church can do about whatever goes on there. Besides, paganism is an accepted faith and these days even satanists are likely to claim their religious rights. Christian clergy can only address what they perceive to be the spiritual or psychological effects of what may or may not be happening.

"I think,' Graham Sykes says, 'that if people dabble with the occult then it affects them — disturbs their psyche. And it can manifest in psycho-kinetic energy. I think they're playing with fire.'

Graham remains unconvinced by the old ghost-stories at Avenbury, suggesting its bad atmosphere may have more to do with what's been happening there *since* it became known as a haunted ruin.

'I think that it's been spiritually damaged by people playing around ... and *that's* why it's an uneasy place. Some places do need to be healed. But first, the *people* need to be healed.'

Which brings us to *The Cure of Souls*.

Avenbury Church

5   Lady of the Bines

A second black pole appeared, rearing hard against the
northern sky, and this one had a short crosspiece like —
his first thought — a gibbet. From it hung something limp
and shrivelled, the skeletal spine of a dead garland;
when he passed between the two poles his bare elbow
brushed against the remains with a dry, papery crackle.
Now he could see the extent of it: dozens of black poles
against the pale night, in lines to either side of him across
the barren ground ... like a site laid out for a mass-crucifixion.

The Cure of Souls

So where do you get your ideas?

As this is acknowledged worldwide as the most blindingly
obvious question aimed at novelists, you'd think people would be
embarrassed to ask it by now. But they aren't, and I actually have
an answer, apart from the one that goes, 'I buy them at night off
this guy in dark glasses and a hoodie on the edge of the Plascarreg
Estate.'

The simple answer is: they come out of the location. You find a
place that looks interesting, examine its history, ancient and recent,
and its folklore, look at its current preoccupations, stir them all
together and add a crime. That's it, really.

The Cure of Souls is set in the Frome Valley of eastern
Herefordshire. Not the most widely known area of the county.
Places quite near to an established tourist area seldom are, and the
Frome Valley will always be in the shadow of the Malverns. Its hills
are discreet and its river is usually unobtrusive. As Lol Robinson
sings,

Looking across the Frome Valley to the Malverns, and its hop fields and old kilns (opposite)

> The River Frome goes nowhere in particular
> It isn't very wide
> There's nothing on the other side.

Actually, Lol may have been using the Frome Valley as a metaphor for the condition of his life at the time. As the novel opens, he's working in the (fictional) village of Knight's Frome — not far from Bishop's Frome and Canon Frome — as assistant to Prof. Levin, the music producer, now assembling his own recording studio there.

Nearby is a converted hop kiln. Not unusual in the Frome Valley, where very few hop kilns these days are used for the hops which were once, thanks to its lush, deep soil, the valley's biggest industry.

Hops

... put the flavour in beer. They are related to nettles and cannabis. The hop plant climbs clockwise around its pole and can reach twenty feet, dying back to the soil every winter. After picking — a major operation — they are dried in hop kilns, which pierce the skyline across the Frome and Lugg Valleys.

It was an intoxicatingly mysterious world, full of arcane terms like hop-crib and hop-devil, and the smell of sulphur. But now, thanks to cheap hops from Off, the Herefordshire industry is in serious decline. Many hopyards have fallen into dereliction. And a derelict hopyard is a spooky place, as Lol discovers in *The Cure of Souls*.

Before cheap hops from Off, the biggest scourge was the voracious Verticillium Wilt, which would put acres of hopyard into quarantine, symbolised in the novel by The Lady of the Bines, a spectral figure haunting hopyards. If you see her, your crop is doomed.

Just as strawberries in the polytunnels further west are now picked mainly by East Europeans, the hops used to be picked by incoming seasonal labour, the Valleys people from South Wales, the Dudleys from the Black Country and — most interesting, as far as this novel is concerned, the gypsies — mainly ...

Romanies

'Romanies respect, sometimes consult the ancestors, but they let the dead lie. Don't ever trust the dead. We have a word ... *mulo* ... the Romani word for a ghost. This word is also used for a vampire. The living dead.

We don't worry about your dead — we'll settle down to sleep in your cemeteries any night of the week. We believe that the Romani dead ... they don't come back for no reason. We're very afraid of the vengeful power of our dead.'

This is Al Boswell talking. In the novel Al is the Romani craftsman behind the famous Boswell Guitar, known these days, thanks to modern marketing, as *The Lute of the Frome*. This much-prized instrument is fashioned from a carefully chosen mixture of woods, which are taken sparingly without the destruction of a single tree. The philosophy of 'borrowing the earth' was borrowed from Patrick Jasper Lee's book, which explains the methods of the *Chovihano*, or Romani shaman. I learned a lot from this book and others possibly out of print now.

For example ... a Romani ghost may appear not at dead of night, but dead of noon. In the brightest sunlight, *the time of no shadows*. A nice twist.

I promise there are no vampires in this, or any of the books. But *The Cure of Souls* does deal with some of the central problems of deliverance: when to exorcise and how far to go, with the atmosphere of a converted hop kiln apparently disturbed as a result of a murder committed there.

Just occasionally a novel happens the other way round, starting not with location but with murder. If it's real murder you're on dangerous ground.

The font at Castle Frome Church

42

6   A Dark Lamp

> Fred's leaning across, apologising to Rose. 'Now I know you
> won't mind, my love, but we gotter drop Jane off in Ledwardine ...'
> *The Lamp of the Wicked*

In this scene, Merrily is dreaming, and it's not the kind of dream anyone needs. But the nightmare grin of the goblinesque mass-murderer Fred West seems destined to become an image out of folklore, swimming up from the darkest undercurrent in rural Herefordshire.

The scale of Fred's evil may never be fully known, the investigation having ended — arguably because of the cost — rather prematurely in my view. But then, what do I know?

More than I feel comfortable with, to be honest. When I first thought of the theme of *The Lamp of the Wicked*, my wife urged me to leave it alone. It was all too recent, the pain too close to the surface.

Fred West was found hanged in his cell before he could stand trial for the murders of women and girls at the home he shared with his wife Rosemary in Cromwell Street, Gloucester. Rose is now serving life for her part in the murders. Fred was a builder and knew how to dispose of bodies under concrete. As a result there were lots of black jokes about patios — the British way of dealing with it.

But, in the end, it was never really dealt with to anyone's satisfaction and its aftermath still hangs like noxious industrial smoke over Gloucester, Herefordshire and the Forest of Dean.

And I kept running into people connected with the case or the West family.

A neighbour of ours recalled some amusing but, with hindsight, slightly sinister stories about a relative of Fred who, apparently, had once worked ... well, very close to where we live. Geoffrey Wansell, who wrote (very much against the clock, so that it could hit the shelves in the wake of Rose's trial) the first and most explicit West biography, *An Evil Love*, would tell me how, after listening to the tapes of Fred's interrogation by police, he would go into the church near his home to try and remove the aura of raw evil they always left behind. Gordon Burn, author of the devastating *Happy like Murderers*, told me he never wanted to deal with a subject this dark again, ever.

But Prof. Bernard Knight, the pathologist who conducted autopsies on several of the victims, pointed out that aspects of the case were still ... unresolved. The implications were extremely sinister, and I decided to go ahead.

Fiction can often say more than speculative non-fiction, but this is the darkest in the series and some readers prefer to avoid it. Personally, I don't think that what the Wests did should ever be forgotten, if only because there's a lot more that needs to come out.

Fred West was born in Much Marcle where, after his arrest, bodies were discovered in Fingerpost field — a lovely spot, actually, not far from the idyllic Kempley Church with its medieval murals. Because he ended up in Gloucester, Fred is usually seen as a low-life city boy; in fact, he was very much a Welsh Border man: practical, independent, self-sufficient. He killed out of expediency and always (to use building trade terminology) 'made good' afterwards.

However, I was determined that *The Lamp of the Wicked* should deal less with the sickening reality of life in Cromwell Street than with the emotional aftermath over a very wide area of western Britain. There are dozens of parents, siblings and boyfriends of missing girls who, not least because the case was too rapidly closed, will never know if they were victims of Fred and Rose. Most people connected with the case believe that many more victims — forty is one informed estimate — may be lying in their unmarked graves.

Lamp is about a man apparently influenced, several years later, by the West murders. It's not, I hope, a gruesome or a sadistic novel as much as an emotional one. But it is dark, and it would have been unfair to burden Much Marcle with a fictional development of the West legend, so I switched the scene to nearby Ross-on-Wye, and the Coughton Valley. Because of the nature of the plot it was necessary to create a new village, Underhowle, named after nearby Howle Hill. However, this is still very much a

Kempley Church chancel arch and chancel (left)
and details of wall paintings (right)

real area, just a few miles from Symonds Yat, which was already linked with a murder by a man known as Black Dai, a Fred West copycat killer from South Wales.

Lamp also deals with the health-damaging, mind-altering effects of living under high-voltage power lines. Massive pylons carrying power to Gloucestershire stalk the Coughton Valley, and I was interested in a theory that linked electricity to so-called alien abduction. In the novel, an environmental activist sees an invisible invasion.

'If we could see all the TV and satellite signals, all the radio waves serving mobile phones, police communications, cab fleets, air networks, the sky would be this kind of poisonous black the whole day long. If we could smell them like exhaust fumes we'd all choke to death. But it's a whole lot more subtle than that. They zip unseen and unfelt through our atmosphere and our bodies and our brains ... the insidious wind that blows through us all ... flesh and tissue and bones ...'

Coughton Valley

The novel also recalls the plague that settled in Ross in 1637, with major loss of life and the town in quarantine, details of which can be found in *The Story of Ross* by Pat Hughes and Heather Hurley. They note a report by Thomas Jenkins which recalls that:

> The dead were buried at night in their wearing apparel in deep graves or pits, numbers at a time ... The bodies were brought in carts and slipped out of the carts into the grave. Good old Vicar Price used to stand on the cross solemnising the funerals by torchlight.

Ross-on-Wye. Above: The Plague Cross and St Mary's Church
Opposite, clockwise from top left: the old lock-up; gazebo tower, the Man of Ross and leaping salmon sculpture;
Wye Street, leading down to the Rope Walk

Later, the minister, Philip Price, led the townsfolk through the streets at 5 am 'chanting a litany with supplications for deliverance', after which the plague is said to have abated.

This is echoed in *The Lamp of the Wicked*, in which the disposal of bodies by night is a recurrent issue. On a less-infected level, the novel also looks at evidence of the Roman town of

Ariconium

which, as local historian Brian Cave wrote, 'remains as a ghost. Though gone in body, its spirit still marks itself upon the landscape.'

Cave thought Ariconium, around what is now Weston under Penyard, near Ross, may have been built to house Roman garrisons protecting iron mines in the nearby Forest of Dean.

You can find it along the old Roman road to Gloucester. Just follow the pylons.

A view in the vicinity of Ariconium

The Forest of Dean

*Old trackway and industrial
remains, Forest of Dean*

7   A Real Creeper

'Mr Holmes, they were the footprints of a gigantic hound.'

But where were they actually planted? On Dartmoor ... or the Welsh Border?

It's over fifty years since Maurice Campbell, chairman at the time of the Sherlock Holmes Society, published a controversial pamphlet, *The Hound of the Baskervilles: Dartmoor or Herefordshire?*

Today, the Sherlock Holmes Society is in no doubt: it's Dartmoor. But the Arthur Conan Doyle Society tends to disagree. The evidence for the spectral Hound having a paw either side of the Border, between Kington and Clyro, is considerable and was explored in the sixth Merrily Watkins book, *The Prayer of the Night Shepherd*. In this novel, a hard-up hotelier, like many before him, is attempting to build a future around the most famous of all Sherlock Holmes stories.

The unnamed Night Shepherd makes a brief appearance in the Baskerville Manuscript shown to Holmes before he comes to the aid of Sir Henry Baskerville, a man who seems to have inherited a curse. In the Manuscript, it's the Night Shepherd who directs friends of the unpleasant Sir Hugo Baskerville to the spot where he's having his throat torn out.

But who directed Sir Arthur Conan Doyle to the Hound?

'I have the idea of a real creeper for the *Strand*,' Conan Doyle wrote in 1901 to Greenough Smith, editor of the London magazine that would print Sherlock Holmes stories ahead of their publication in book form.

There was one stipulation, however, Doyle said. 'I must do it with my friend Fletcher Robinson.'

Robinson, much younger, at 28, than Doyle, and from Devon, had entertained the great man, during a golfing holiday in Norfolk, with the legend of a spectral hound. Doyle was inspired.

So which legend *was* this? As far as the Holmes Society was concerned, it had to be the story of Sir Richard Cabell, the most hated man on Dartmoor, and his revenant canine companion. When Doyle and Robinson went to Devon to research the novel, the coachman who drove them around was one Harry Baskerville.

Case closed? Apparently not. The most recent Conan Doyle biography, *Teller of Tales* by Daniel Stashower, points out that Greenough Smith later recalled Robinson saying he'd found the legend in 'a Welsh guide book'. And the proposed title of the book was disclosed by Conan Doyle in a letter to his mother in Scotland before he and Robinson had been to Dartmoor or, presumably, met Harry Baskerville.

However, Welsh and Herefordshire guidebooks, to this day, often re-tell the story of ...

Black Vaughan of Hergest

Hergest Court should not be confused with Hergest Croft, where the gardens are open to the public. Hergest Court, a much bleaker-looking place in a more exposed location, doesn't do gardens.

I first went there in the late 1980s to record a programme for BBC Radio Wales. The tenant farmer at the time, John Williams, remembered the 'prickly feeling' that went up his back when he once heard, from the hall, what sounded like the patter of huge paws in an upstairs room. Later, he said, he saw a hound-like shadow passing in front of him towards the inner hall.

You'll still find people in Kington who won't go down the lane to Hergest after dark. Bob Jenkins, journalist, historian and Kington oracle, told me about a man cycling to work at Kington Camp during World War Two.

'Near Hergest Court, he saw this enormous hound which he'd never seen before and never saw again. The hound had huge eyes — that's what impressed him. He had a feeling that there was something that just wasn't real about it.'

Hergest Court

54

Kington. Above: The Square (left) and Baptist Chapel glimpsed (right); Below: The church

The Vaughan tomb, Kington Church

To this day, you can hear accounts of psychic disturbance at Hergest Court, and it all seems to be down to Black Vaughan — Thomas Vaughan, who lived at the Court when it was much bigger and more fortified than the present sawn-off farmhouse.

The events in the Baskerville Manuscript take place during The Great Rebellion, the English Civil War. Black Vaughan — so called, apparently, merely because of the colour of his hair — took part in the previous civil conflict, the Wars of the Roses. Vaughan changed sides, from Lancaster to York (changing sides comes easily to border people; it's about survival) and was said to have been killed at a battle near Banbury. His headless body was brought back to Kington, to be buried next to his wife Ellen Gethin ('the terrible'), who has her own legend. They now lie side by side in a rather spooky tomb in the Vaughan Chapel in Kington Parish Church.

Vaughan has been described as a notorious tyrant, although there's nothing in history to support this. It was only after death that he began to measure up to Hugo Baskerville's level of infamy, when a spectral hound was also seen, its appearances heralding death in the Vaughan family. The ghost of Vaughan himself began to exhibit signs of revenant-rage, rampaging through Kington, turning over farmers' carts and disrupting church services by manifesting as a bull. Fairly soon, nobody wanted to come to Kington Market and the town's economy began to suffer.

It was decided, at this stage, that Vaughan needed to be properly exorcised.

This was a big job that took twelve priests. Ella Mary Leather's *The Folklore of Herefordshire* tells how Vaughan appeared during the ritual, insisting he had now become a devil. Eventually subdued, after a lot of shouting and extinguishing of candles, his spirit was shrunk, confined to a snuff box — local historian Alan Lloyd suggests this was actually a candle-snuffer box — and buried under a stone at the bottom of the pool in front of Hergest Court.

Only the Hound remained, as a harbinger of death in the Vaughan family and a spectral watchdog around Hergest, where no Vaughan has resided since the death of the Rev. Silvanus Vaughan in 1706.

The final problem

So is it Dartmoor or the Welsh Border?

I think Conan Doyle's hound is a mongrel. This is what novelists do — pinch material from different sources, muddying its origins. But, as far as the hound's pedigree goes, the balance of probability falls towards the Border.

The original Baskervilles were Norman barons who came over after the conquest, building castles at Eardisley in Herefordshire and Aberedw across the border in Radnorshire. Their descendants owned the mansion Clyro Court, now the Baskerville Hall Hotel. The pub in the village of Clyro has always been The Baskerville Arms. If you look at the family tree of the Vaughans of Hergest you'll find evidence of intermarriage with the Baskervilles of Clyro.

After publication of *The Prayer of the Night Shepherd* raked up the embers of the old argument and a story in the Daily Telegraph had Hound fans snapping at each other in the paper's letters column, I had an email from Christopher Roden, of the Arthur Conan Doyle Society, who explained,

> Conan Doyle's first wife, Louise, whom he married in 1885, was one of the Hawkins of Minsterworth family. When he married her, and until her death, Louise was receiving an annuity from her brother Joseph's farms, the Bettws and Whitehall farms at Clyro. A neighbouring owner was Thomas Baskerville Mynors Baskerville, and the Hawkins farms were eventually sold to Ralph Hopton Baskerville in 1907, following Louise's death in 1906.

It's inconceivable, given such a close connection, that Conan Doyle wouldn't have visited the area at some stage.

It seems to be quite impossible that ACD would not have known the legend of Black Vaughan's demon dog.

Vaughans also married Hawkinses.

Around the same time, the late Geoffrey Hopton, last of the Hopton/Baskervilles in Clyro, told me that his grandmother's understanding of the situation had been that Conan Doyle did indeed know about

Black Vaughan and had asked if he could use the name Baskerville in his novel, as it had more resonance. The Baskervilles said yes ... as long as he located the novel somewhere else.

This was confirmed in *Out of the Shadows: The Untold Story of Conan Doyle's first family*, by a descendant, Georgina Doyle.

The final evidence, for me, is the coincidence of names. Apart from Baskerville itself, there's Mortimer — it's Dr Mortimer who first brings the problem to the attention of Sherlock Holmes. The Mortimers, of course, were for many years the most powerful Norman family in the Welsh Marches.

There's also Stapleton, the naturalist, a key character in the novel and the name of a hamlet just beyond Presteigne, a few miles from Kington.

So where's Baskerville Hall?

Although there's evidence in the cellars of an earlier building on the site, Clyro Court, former home of the Baskervilles, now the Baskerville Hall Hotel, is Victorian and therefore unlikely to be Conan Doyle's model. It could be that Baskerville Hall is on Dartmoor, but if you're looking for a Welsh Border house which fits the image, it's worth investigating

Kinnersley Castle

This Welsh border stronghold, a few miles from Clyro on the Herefordshire side, was held for generations by the de la Bere family, two generations of whom are entombed in the Church of St Cosmas and St Damian at Stretford.

But in the mid 16th century it became the property of Roger Vaughan, MP for Radnorshire, and grandson of Black Vaughan himself, who spent a fortune turning a Norman castle into a state-of-the-art Tudor mansion, with tall leaded windows and a four-storey central tower.

If you want to feel the power of the Vaughans, this is the place. Over a fireplace is the emblem of the Vaughans, a child with a snake wound around his neck. (It's been speculated that this is what gave Conan Doyle the idea for *The Speckled Band*, the one where ... well, I won't spoil it if you haven't read it.) And there's a ceiling with the heads of hounds, dragons and a green man.

There are yew trees outside, close to the castle. There may have been, as at Baskerville Hall, a yew alley ...

De Bere tomb, Church of St Cosmas and Damian, Stretford

Kinnersley Castle

It doesn't end …

In 1987, Jenny Vaughan, a businesswoman from the Midlands, came to Kington with a friend to investigate her family history. She didn't, fortunately perhaps, see the hound. But she did see a bull in the church where, you'll remember, the angry spirit of Black Vaughan was said to take taurine form. I talked to Jenny, for radio, inside the church, some months later.

It made very convincing radio.

> The inside of his nostrils — this was one of the most vivid things — were very, very red, like a racehorse when it's just stopped running. And it was wet. It was dripping moisture or something on to the ground. It was as though it was hanging in strings … I'm a hard-headed business person but I can't deny it. I've seen it.

Over at Hergest Court, the hauntings, it seems, have never gone away. Tenants regularly report disturbances.

As for Hergest pool, where the spirit of Black Vaughan is supposed to lie in its snuff box, Roy Palmer records in his *Herefordshire Folklore* that when there were attempts to fill in the pool some years ago the project was abandoned after the water began to bubble ominously.

A few years ago, when the water level dropped, it was decided the pool should be cleaned out, and a large stone became visible. Historian Alan Lloyd thought this might be a good opportunity to find out if there was any kind of container underneath it and tried to persuade local farmers with mechanical diggers to check it out.

Nobody was prepared to go near. I don't even think Gomer Parry would've done it.

Stanner Rocks

Much of the action in *Prayer* takes place at the Stanner Hall Hotel, close to Stanner Rocks, said to be the oldest rocks (over 700 million years old) in Wales.

The rocks can be seen from the edge of the Kington bypass on the Welsh side, bulging out of the hillside foliage like stone age sculpture. A combination of geography and air currents means that some spots up there have an almost Mediterranean climate, and Fred Slater, in *The Nature of Central Wales*, describes the rocks as a 'botanical jewel,' because of the rare — and even unique — plant species found there.

As for the Stanner Hall Hotel ... that's roughly in the vicinity of the less decrepit Dunfield Manor, now a conference centre. Local people insist Arthur Conan Doyle once stayed there.

It doesn't seem to be haunted.

*Stanner Rocks
near Kington*

8   A place to die for

Merrily felt very small and exposed.

She was wearing jeans and a green fleece with a torn pocket. She
had a canvas shoulder bag with her cigarettes inside and her phone.
Around her neck was a chain with a tiny gold cross on it that was
hidden by the neck of her grey T-shirt.

Disoriented in an old town like a pop-up book, coming at her
from all angles in wedges of carrot-coloured antique brick and twisting
timbers and thrusting gables ...

The Smile of a Ghost

This is a novel about ... well, ghosts, kind of, but mainly about obsession. It's now slightly notorious for (a
couple of years before the tragic Bridgend epidemic of 2008) having a theme of localised teenage suicide,
linked, in this case, to a famous fall from the Hanging Tower of Ludlow Castle in south Shropshire.

Ludlow is a town which usually attracts less fatal obsession, but obsession nonetheless. People visit it
and just *have* to live there — not only, perhaps, because of the recent boom in fancy restaurants, or even the
fact that Ludlow is frequently named as the most beautiful medieval town in Britain. It could be something
far more elusive, because it goes back centuries. Even three hundred years ago, the town had a reputation as
a resort ... somewhere it was good just to be.

In the novel, the notoriously gothic singer, Bell Pepper, known as Belladonna, moves to Ludlow and,
for reasons which, if you haven't read the novel, you wouldn't want me to explain here, begins to roam its
streets and passageways at night with a candle-lamp, like a ghost.

However, the novel's, and the town's, real ghost may be someone else.

Marion de la Bruyere

There are two ways out of that tower, and I took the wrong one at first
and came up against some steps that led nowhere any more, a blank
wall, and that was horrifying, as if whichever way I went I'd come up

against a wall that hadn't been there when I went in. Imagination, in these situations, becomes so unbelievably powerful. So I scrambled back down and back into the chamber and … well … that's when I saw her.

Bernie Dunmore, Bishop of Hereford, *The Smile of a Ghost*

A lady of the castle is how Marion is usually described, which, when you think about it, could mean anything. She was probably very young when she died.

This was in the 12th century, the reign of Henry II, whose predecessor, Stephen, had given control of Ludlow Castle to a Breton knight, Joce de Dinan, who may have left his name to Dinham, the sloping community between the castle and the River Teme.

Ludlow Castle is probably the most impressive medieval stronghold along the Welsh border. It has many royal connections, and was once the military HQ for Wales. In a honeyed light, it looks deceptively mellow. Except, possibly, for the Hanging Tower.

The baronial de Lacy family, big in the area, had coveted this castle for some time, and the Lacy/Dinan conflict had led to the capture of a young knight, Arnold de Lisle. While imprisoned in the castle, Arnold formed a relationship with Marion de la Bruyere, who helped him escape down a rope or possibly knotted sheets. Unfortunately she then let him back up by rope ladder and, during their rapturous reunion, a whole bunch of heavily-armed de Lacy men shot up the ladder and took the castle. Soon afterwards, there was much slaughter and destruction in the town to make it clear that de Lacy was now in control.

Views of Ludlow Castle. This page: The Round Chapel with part of the northern range behind
Opposite, clockwise from top left: part of the northern range; the northern façade of the Judge's Lodgings;
entrance to the keep which led to the rooms above the gateway in the Judge's Lodgings;
the entrance steps to the Great Hall. Opposite: looking over the castle from the tower of St Laurence's Church

When she saw what she'd done, the remorseful Marion killed Arnold with his own sword and then, fearing either repercussions from Joce or gang-rape by de Lacy's heavies, threw herself from the highest window in the Hanging Tower. It was said that her final anguished screams could be heard for years afterwards before they were reduced to a breathing sound. In *A Gazetteer of British Ghosts*, Peter Underwood recalled a Ludlow man, Mr J. Didlick, 'who told me that the sounds might be likened to those made by someone in very deep sleep'.

So maybe she's at peace now.

I couldn't find Mr Didlick, but the Hanging Tower may be viewed from inside the castle, now owned by the Earl of Powis, whose home castle at Welshpool is in far better repair.

But, for a more dramatic — and cheaper — view of the tower, follow the public footpath to the right of the castle, as you approach it from the town centre. You'll eventually arrive at the yew tree under Marion's window, the subject of the chapter entitled *Tonguing the Yew*, in *The Smile of a Ghost*.

(Health and Safety warning: don't tongue the yew. Yews are very poisonous.)

Anyway, this is a significant point on Bell Pepper's ghostwalk, which you might prefer to start from the other end of town, beginning in ...

St Leonard's Graveyard

Possibly my all-time favourite cemetery can be reached from the bottom of Corve Street by following the path alongside the former church, which now serves as a printing and copying workshop. The disused graveyard itself — and it's fair to say not everybody thinks this is a good thing — has been allowed to become atmospherically overgrown as a wildlife haven. It will lead you to some nicely-framed and unexpectedly green views of the castle across the town.

In fact, it's possible to walk from here to the castle avoiding all prominent streets and rarely encountering, even in high season, too many people ... although ghosts can't be ruled out as you wander through the yards of one-time coaching inns, up and down stone steps, along narrow alleyways, catching ribbons of conversation through open back doors as whole centuries seem to drop away.

You need to stop in the Linney, the steep, narrow street backing on to the castle's curtain wall before curving down to the River Teme. All very clean and refined now but it's easy to imagine medieval human detritus in full foetid flow down the earthen gutters to the river.

You will, by now, have passed through the shadow of the church sometimes called the Beacon of the Marches.

Above: St Leonard's graveyard
Opposite. Top left: The Feathers Hotel; lower right: The Reader's House;
together with examples of carvings on Ludlow's buildings

The Church of St Laurence

I once stayed in the centre of Ludlow for two months, while starting a new job, and the church clock awoke me every hour on the hour all through the night. It's been quietened now, which is a shame in a way. But the church is still as big a presence in the old town as the castle, and its foundations may be even older, built, as they were, out of a Neolithic mound, presumably the *low* in Ludlow.

St Laurence's, as you can see from the amazing vantage point at Whitcliffe — don't miss this view — is the centre of the wheel of Ludlow. If you have the stamina and a head for heights, you can climb to the top of the tower, scene of the climax of *Smile*, and take in dizzying views of the castle, the town and Clee Hill beyond. The vertiginous should at least check out

Top: part of the ceiling in St Laurence's Church
Bottom: The Butter Market, St Laurence's Church tower and Bodenham's
Opposite: misericords in St Laurence's Church

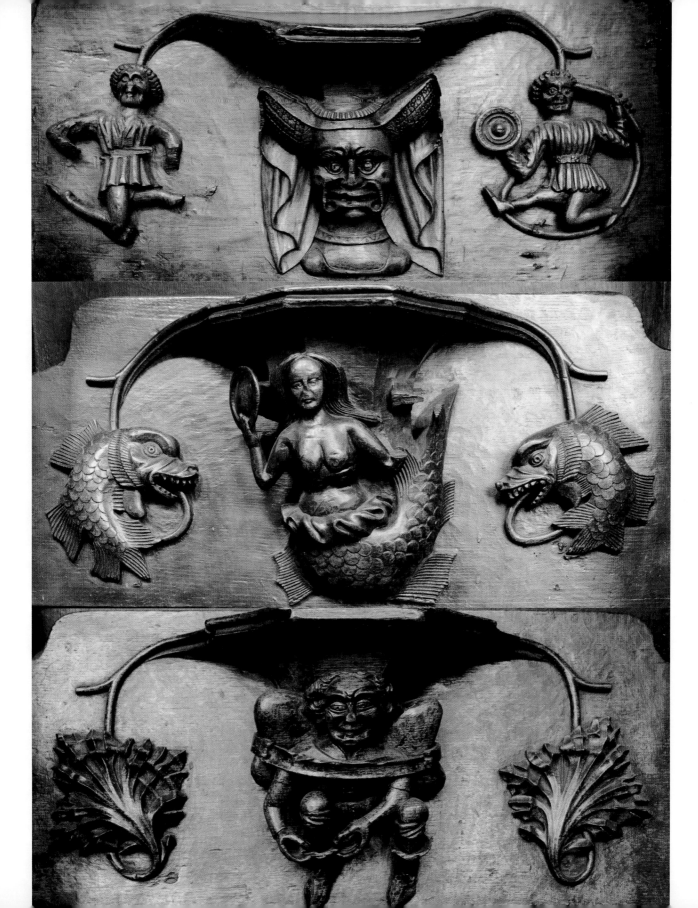

the Palmers' Window inside the church, which commemorates

The Palmers' Guild

A palmer was a medieval pilgrim to the Holy Land who brought back a palm frond as evidence of having done the trip. The Palmers' Guild was mystically linked to the cult of King Edward the Confessor and to St John. You can get an idea of all this possibly-wishful thinking in the impressive 15th-century eight-paned Palmers' stained-glass window. More than just a collection of 'what we did on our pilgrimage' snaps.

The Guild, consisting mainly of wealthy businessmen, was formed to employ priests whose main function was to pray for the souls of Guild members and their families. In those days, buying a stairway to heaven was as legitimate as taking out a pension fund and, indeed, the Guild also fulfilled a similar role in supporting members who fell on hard times.

It's difficult, without one of those *look away now* moments, to explain the significance, in this novel, of the Palmers' Guild. But it's worth noting that, while there were similar guilds all over Britain, Ludlow's achieved national prominence.

Palmers' Guild window,
St Laurence's Church

9   Music of the Spheres

'Drivers reckoned they swerved to avoid a ghost,' Spicer said.

His tone hadn't altered and his eyes remained limpid. A wood pigeon's hollow call was funnelled out of the valley.

'That took a while to come, didn't it?' Merrily said.

The Remains of an Altar

Altar begins — and perhaps ends — with a ghost story, and the idea for the novel began with a real one.

A few years ago, villagers at Stoke Lacy, in eastern Herefordshire, came to believe that the road through their community was haunted, following a series of unexplained road accidents.

British Camp and Midsummer Hill from the west

Most accidents involve more than one vehicle, maybe one driver swerving to avoid another. In Stoke Lacy, vehicles were leaving the road in isolation, drivers saying it felt as if someone else was moving the steering wheel. It happened so many times that an exorcism was suggested, and there was consultation with the man who was standing in, at the time, for Merrily Watkins.

However, the deliverance minister for Hereford had a problem with it. For a start, there was no back-story — no famous death-crash in the past, no suggestion of an unquiet spirit which might benefit from a Requiem Eucharist, or even an imprint or place-memory. In the end he was unconvinced and took no action.

The only solution was offered by members of the British Association of Dowsers, who surveyed the road with rods and pendulums and concluded that the problem had been caused by the siting of a millennial stone in a wood which they suggested may have been disrupting the energy flow, causing a reflex reaction in the motorists.

Either way, it made me think about unexplained road accidents, and that's how *The Remains of an Altar* begins — although not in Stoke Lacy — as Merrily Watkins is called in to investigate similar, if more extreme, accidents in the village of Wychehill.

To find the general area of this troubled community, take the main road north-east from Ledbury and turn left by the hotel near the British Camp car-park. This puts you in the Malvern Hills ... which really are the remains of an altar.

We live just below the Black Mountains, and the Malverns are our easterly horizon. It's clear to anyone who lives or walks or drives around this area that there's a link between the Black Mountains of Wales and the Malverns (from the Welsh *moel bryn* — bald hill) of England. Two great, sacred shelves of rock enclosing Herefordshire's landscaped garden of lush pastures, orchards and hopyards.

The English Heritage publication *The Malvern Hills, an Ancient Landscape*, by Mark Bowden, with David Field and Helen Winton, confirmed what I'd always felt: these hills, with the lofty earthworks of Herefordshire Beacon and Midsummer Hill, *were* the remains of an altar. Sacred. Untouchable. Full of earth energy and the lifeforce of water.

The Victorian spa of Great Malvern tapped into the healing power of mineral waters, but there was something here that was clearly recognised in Celtic and pre-Celtic times, when the earthworks were taking shape.

And later, inbetween the Celtic and Victorian eras, 'it is tempting,' say the authors of *An Ancient Landscape*, 'to consider the Malvern Hills as a "ritual landscape" in the medieval period as much as in the

Little Malvern Priory

prehistoric periods'. The book goes on to identify the hills as a magnet for early Christian hermits, spiritually challenged by the desolation and that sense of exposure, not only to the elements but to 'ancient practices and spirits'.

Out of Celtic Christian hermitages came the spiritual strongholds of Great Malvern and Little Malvern priories: '... the priorities are not ordinary parish churches but rather the bases of religious "elite forces".'

Which somehow confirmed my idea of having an ex-SAS man as the vicar of Wychehill, letting me into some of the legends of The Regiment, based in Hereford.

But it was never going to be easy, or even possible, to write a novel set in the Malvern Hills without involving another legend — Britain's most famous composer.

I didn't know all that much about Sir Edward Elgar beyond the usual clichés: Master of the King's Music, Pomp and Circumstance, making Britain mightier yet ... This stiff, slightly aloof establishment figure wheeled out annually for The Last Night of the Proms.

However, after a few months' serious research, I was looking at a very different person: Ed, the Worcester piano-tuner's son who married above his class. Ed, the paranoid perfectionist, insecure, depressive, often in despair over his work. A man who actually loved *the country* more than The Country. Who wrote brilliant music but is too often associated with words he *didn't* write. Whose high-Catholicism was sometimes challenged by an instinctive paganism. Whose friend and confidante, for some years, seems to have been his daughter's white rabbit, Peter.

And then there was another friend ...

For some years, Edward Elgar, the composer, and Alfred Watkins, who discovered leys, were neighbours in Hereford.

This isn't widely known. But then, why would it be? While Hereford's connection with Elgar is always being underlined in the city and the pages of the *Hereford Times*, Watkins, who was born here and served Hereford all his working life, still gets more recognition outside. Far more.

It's bloody criminal, really. Sorry ... I keep going on about this. There should be an Alfred Watkins Museum and visitor centre in Hereford, but I expect the Establishment is worried about attracting undesirables with walking boots and dowsing rods.

Anyway, Elgar's famous residence, Plas Gwyn, now flats, is on the corner of the road which led to Watkins' house, The Vineyard, where he lived before moving into the centre of the city.

Ed and Alfred were born within a year of one another. Both were into photography and gadgets. Elgar had a dark-room at Plas Gwyn and would have been fascinated by Watkins' various photographic inventions, including the first light-meter.

And then there was the countryside. Both were members of the Woolhope Naturalists' Field Club. Both were drawn to a pastoral, very British kind of mysticism.

Why is this connection never referred to in major biographies of either of them?

I don't know, but it seemed like an interesting thread for the novel.

Plas Gwyn

British Camp (with its Norman motte visible on the skyline) and Edward Elgar

I was haunted particularly by Elgar's *Cello Concerto* which, although it was written after he'd moved away from Malvern, seems to reflect the evening light and shadows on the hills and the *movement* of the hills. It was the *Cello Concerto*, on an early gramophone record, that drifted around the room where Elgar lay dying and which he whistled to a friend before he said,

> If ever you're walking on the Malvern Hills and hear that, don't be
> frightened ... it's only me.

And it *is* him. He haunts those hills. Especially Herefordshire Beacon with the earthworks on top like a dented sandwich cake.

Elgar's choral epic, *Caractacus*, recalls the legend (long ago discredited) that this was the site of the Ancient British hero's last stand against the Romans. The music is full of numinous shapes in the woods and druidic blood-ritual ... and it goes way over the top, thanks to the librettist's determination to turn it into a hymn to a British Empire far wider than Rome's puny effort.

'I did suggest we should dabble in patriotism in the Finale,' Elgar wrote later, 'when, lo!, the worder, instead of merely paddling his feet goes & gets naked & wallows in it ...'

All Elgar wallowed in was the mystery and the energy of the countryside, as he pedalled along the lanes around his home at Birchwood on his beloved bike Mr Phoebus — commemorated in the bronze sculpture on the cathedral green in Hereford — not far, as it happens, from Alfred Watkins' last home. Ed is leaning on Mr Phoebus peering up at the Cathedral, with big trees on either side, and on the plinth it says,

This is what I get every day. The trees are singing my music — or am I singing theirs?

Elgar statue,
Cathedral Close, Hereford

This page, opposite and overleaf: oaks on the Malverns

Elgar loved trees, was moved and inspired by them. While living in the south of England he once took his friend and musical collaborator Algernon Blackwood, ritual magician and author of classic ghost stories, including *The Man Whom the Trees Loved*, to see some oaks near his home which were said to be monks bewitched. He loved that story.

So it seemed inconceivable that Elgar, with that passion for trees and the interest in druidic ritual displayed in *Caractacus*, was not intimately familiar with the

Whiteleafed Oak

You'll find the oak — well, several of them — at the end of the Malvern Hills, almost exactly at the meeting point of the counties of Herefordshire, Worcestershire and Gloucestershire, the three counties that come together for the annual Three Choirs Festival, for which Elgar composed some of his finest sacred music.

This is also the centre of the circle of Perpetual Choirs, which I first read about in the works of John Michell, the writer who rediscovered Alfred Watkins in the 1960s and raised him to a new level of international fame in books including *The View over Atlantis*.

Essentially, Michell developed what Watkins himself had only

hinted at — the idea that alignments of old stones and mounds and other landscape patterns were the remains of an ancient knowledge far more advanced than history recognises ... reflecting a universal harmony most of us can no longer perceive.

The novel forms a curious link between all this and Elgar's most complex and profound choral work, *The Dream of Gerontius*, from Cardinal Newman's account of what happens to a man's soul after death ... a journey into the formal Roman Catholic afterlife with all its angelic bureaucracy. Not exactly easy-listening, often emotional and strangely tense.

And there's one moment that shoots right up your spine. A dangerous moment which the composer, conscious of sacrilege, nearly bottled, and ... this is where you need to read the novel, but it builds into an exploration of the ancient science of Pythagoras and the seductive theories of cosmic harmony and the Music of the Spheres.

And suppose Elgar *had* spent time at Whiteleafed Oak while agonising — and he really *did* agonise — over *Gerontius*?

Whiteleafed Oak is a hamlet, up a narrow lane from Hollybush, not far from Eastnor Castle. In a glass case on the village green you may find a curious little diagram related to *Harmonic Convergences* (or something). All a bit New Agey, but the significance gradually becomes apparent to Merrily Watkins in the course of *The Remains of an Altar*, as she and Lol Robinson learn about the Perpetual Choirs and meet the eccentric composer Tim Loste.

You can only reach the actual oaks on foot. It's about half a mile from the houses, across the fields. The original great oak, said to be a centre of Druid worship, at the end of a processional trail, is long gone, but its successor has been chosen. Amongst its boughs, in the wrinkles of its vast bole, you'll find offerings — ribbons and shiny things — left by recent pilgrims.

Now observe the newly-exposed views to the landmarks of the three counties.

And listen ...

10   Ghosts and Templars

> Outside, a wind had arisen, chattering amongst dead chrysanths
> in a grave pot. Merrily pulled the church keys from her shoulder
> bag. The Master House key poked out and she thrust it back ...
>
> *The Fabric of Sin*

Research for *The Fabric of Sin* uncovered the fact that not only had the Knights Templar church at Garway been visited by the — almost certainly — greatest-ever writer of ghost stories, M.R. James, but that *something happened to him there.*

Something disturbing, referred to obliquely but tantalisingly in a letter to his Herefordshire friend, Gwen MacBride.

It was a gift.

Everything in Garway seemed like a gift. Its history, its folklore, its very strange church, its dovecote with 666 dove-holes ... even the names of its pubs argued that something curious was, and may still be, at work in this landscape, a kind of inland peninsula of England dropping down to the River Monnow, on the other side of which is Wales.

It's not easy setting a novel in a very small community which actually exists. While I've always identified real towns and a few larger villages, I get cold feet about inflicting murder, feuds and iffy history on a tiny community where people and houses could easily be (wrongly) identified.

M.R. James

Garway, though ... with Garway, there was no way around it. And it helped that the suggestion for a Garway novel came from a very long-established and respected local family, and all the people I spoke to were well aware of what I was doing and were *still* helpful. It was necessary to create the Master House, incorporating elements of other dwellings and acting as a catalyst for the floating weirdness, but most of the rest you can visit.

But let's approach this place, initially, in the company of the writer and academic, Montague Rhodes James.

M.R. James (1862–1936)

This man is an example, still, for everybody who aspires to write a ghost story.

Although, of course, M.R. James didn't actually do ghosts. He mainly did ... things. Entities. Malevolent, terrifying entities. Think of what was inside the ash tree in the story of that name. The 'lungless laugh' from *A Warning to the Curious*. And, most important in the *Fabric of Sin* context, the 'face of crumpled linen' from *Oh Whistle and I'll Come to you, My Lad*.

A serious scholar, like several of his protagonists, Monty James, son of a clergyman in Suffolk, became provost of Eton and King's College, Cambridge, studied old manuscripts, church architecture, stained glass ... tombs.

Dore Abbey with (opposite) two of its wall paintings

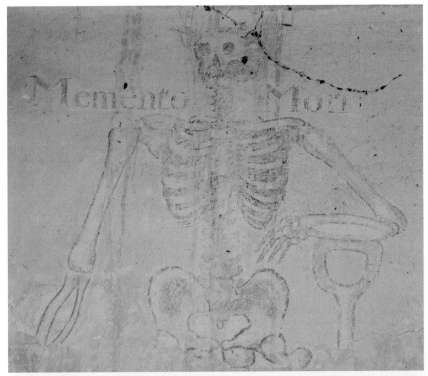

And spent a lot of time in Herefordshire where he stayed with the widow of his friend James McBryde, who illustrated his first volume of ghost stories and died far too young. From 1906, Gwendolen McBryde and her daughter, Jane, lived near Kilpeck. Gwen seems to have been devoted to Monty in a platonic sort of way. He'd spend relaxing holidays with the McBrydes and became guardian to Jane, who displayed graphic skills from an early age and was also very fond of things emerging from gaping tombs.

Monty was especially fond of the McBrydes' second home in Herefordshire, from which he attended services at Dore Abbey. In her book, *Letters to a Friend*, Gwendolen recalled him reading the lesson in 'his fine, slightly plaintive voice ... It always gave me an unreal feeling, as if some saint held forth to lesser creatures and birds.'

Although he said Hereford Cathedral may have been one of the locations behind *The Stalls of Barchester*, the only M.R. James story set wholly in Herefordshire was *A View from a Hill*, the one involving strange visions seen through a particular pair of binoculars.

Oh Whistle and I'll Come to you, My Lad involves the ruins of a Knights Templar preceptory. In the story, this is in Monty's native Suffolk, probably Felixstowe.

But some of the best preserved and most mysterious Templar remains in the country are to be found at Garway.

For more than seven centuries, this order of medieval warrior monks has been gathering mystique like fairy dust. Established in the 12th century to protect Christian pilgrims, The Order of the Poor Knights of Christ and the Temple of Solomon got rich quick, having become the first international bankers and — allegedly — discovered lost treasures on the site of the famous temple in Jerusalem where they were based.

Were they the guardians of the Holy Grail? And what *was* the Holy Grail? According to the cult 1980s bestseller, *The Holy Blood and the Holy Grail*, later fictionalised in *The Da Vinci Code*, the Grail legends obscure the bloodline of Jesus and Mary Magdalene, who apparently were an item.

Or not. In *The Fabric of Sin*, I left all this alone and concentrated on the Templars themselves and, particularly, their last Grand Master, Jacques de Molay, who is said to have spent time in Garway.

You can read about all this in Audrey Tapper's *Knights Templar & Hospitaller in Herefordshire*, which collects all the known facts about Garway and the other local Templar sites, principally at Dinmore, so I'm not going to pinch Audrey's research here. Anyway, novels let you *develop* the facts.

This page and opposite: Garway Church, with a detail of the chancel arch

The Church of St Michael
(Yes, another one)

Not much has actually changed in Garway since the Templar church was handed over to their successors, the Hospitallers. You can still see the remains of the circular nave, built in imitation of the Church of the Holy Sepulchre in Jerusalem. The sandstone tower, which seems to wear a kind of sardonic little smile and was originally separated from the body of the church, was also built by the Templars, whose stone coffin lids you'll find in window ledges and the chancel steps.

Templars everywhere. Still. And what exactly are those golden figures which appear in the picture I snapped when the red curtain was drawn across the nave (see page 13)?

Garway Church is small, unspoiled but *never* cosy. An experienced dowser, exploring the interior with Sir Richard Heygate during research for Richard's book, with Philip Carr-Gomm, *English Magic*, in 2008, said he'd experienced a shattering sense of evil in the area of the piscina, once used to wash the communion chalice.

Personally, I've never detected evil here, but there's certainly a pervading air of secrecy. I was in the church one dappled autumn morning, with my wife, Carol, and local historian Sue Rice, when the dowser and Egyptologist John Ward perambulated the tower and suggested there was a secret room in which something had been kept. Outside, he arranged us all around a field where he'd dowsed the outline of a vanished building.

There's a lot still to be found here.

On the edge of farm buildings behind the church, the holy spring trickles, overhung by small, ribbony offerings — perhaps the water supply which first commended this place as a religious settlement.

Follow the stream to the edge of the churchyard, and there, among the farm buildings you can see the columbarium, like a kiln.

The dovecote. Probably built by the Templars and improved by the Hospitallers. One of the finest, best-preserved medieval dovecotes

84

in Britain, its dove-chambers numbering an enigmatic 666. The Number of the Beast ... possibly. Nobody knows why it has this exact number of chambers, but the stone plinth in the middle is unlikely to be an altar to Satan.

This is where Merrily and Jane have that first fateful meeting with Mrs Morningwood, the alternative therapist and possibly one of the Nine Witches of Garway (we'll get to them).

Meanwhile, back in the church, on the left side of the chancel arch, you need to meet someone else.

Garway: The church (opposite),
The Holy Well (right) and Columbarium (below)

The Green Man

Examples of the Green Man are found in churches all over Britain, with several in Herefordshire. A male face peers through twigs and leaves, teeth clenched around them. The *foliate face* is normally considered a pagan fertility symbol, but nobody really knows and nobody knows, either, why it's found in Christian churches.

Garway's Green Man however, is subtly different. As Sue Rice has pointed out, whatever is issuing from his mouth seems more like a cord with tassles than foliage ... and the cord is associated with Baphomet, the bearded head which the Knights Templar were said to have venerated and which was later turned into a scarily androgynous symbol sometimes connected with black magic.

The Green Man at Garway Church

The image of the Green Man filters through history and has royal connections. Charles II, peering through the branches of an oak tree while hiding from his enemies, is one example. The latest one, of course, is the Prince of Wales, champion of organic farming, energy conservation and alternative therapies, who may, apparently — given the problems encountered by the two previous King Charleses — decide to adopt another name on accession to the throne.

The Prince's business, The Duchy of Cornwall owns many thousands of acres in Herefordshire and acquired the Harewood Estate, only a few miles from Garway, where a working hamlet is being rebuilt, along with a large house.

The Harewood Estate also has a Knights Templar chapel.

It seemed reasonable that the Duchy, which owns many farms, should buy the Master House, so called because of its connection with Jacques de Molay, last Grand Master of the order.

De Molay was publicly burned in Paris after charges of heresy and borderline satanic worship were laid against the Templars by the King of France, Philip the Fair, and his friend the Pope. The basis of these charges seems to lie in the fact that the Templars were very rich and the King of France needed the money, but Baphomet doesn't seem to have been an invention of the prosecution and it's arguable

Jacques de Molay

that some Templar communities had become corrupted. My feeling is that de Molay himself, while a bit of an operator, was probably on the side of the angels. The climax of *The Fabric of Sin*, in which Jacques is remembered, occurs on the 700th anniversary of his death.

But let's return to M.R. James who, during a holiday in Herefordshire, went one day, with either Jane or Gwendolen or both of them, to visit Garway Church. A memorable visit, which he referred to later in a letter to Gwendolen:

> We must have offended somebody or something at Garway, I think. Probably we took it too much for granted, in speaking of it, that we should be able to do exactly as we pleased. Next time we shall know better. There is no doubt that it is a very rum place and needs careful handling.

The sign for The Garway Moon

Now, it could be that they simply left a gate open and were pursued by a farmer with a stick. And yet it's very much the sort of thing people say in an M.R. James ghost story. 'Somebody or something.' And it's the *place* that he describes as rum and in need of careful handling.

This figures.

M.R. James was often asked if he actually believed in ghosts and his careful reply was that he was prepared to consider the evidence.

In putting *Fabric* together, I looked at the plot of *Oh Whistle ...* which does involve an actual whistle, found by a visiting academic in the remains of those Knights Templar ruins in Suffolk. When he blows it he summons the wind ... and something else. Something made out of rumpled bedclothes, with a face of crumpled linen.

As recorded by Ella Mary Leather, whistling up the wind was once common practice amongst

A sign for The Sun in Garway, in fact not the inn but a one time shop that went by the same name

Herefordshire farmers, to bring on a winnowing breeze. From Mrs Leather, too, I learned that Garway was one of the last places to maintain the *watch after death*, in which the whole household sat up all night when someone died on the premises. A pewter plate of salt was placed on the body, with a candle in its centre. I started to interweave these stories to seek out an explanation of Monty's reference to a *rum place*.

And it *is* a rum place. It did have four pubs, all linked to the heavens — the Sun, the Moon (the only one still open), the Globe and the Seven Stars.

And it did have that old saying,

There'll be nine witches from the bottom
of Orcop to the end of Garway Hill as
long as water flows ...

Candidates for the Nine are identified to this day.

11　The Uncoiling of the Serpent

The landscape itself was throwing off centuries like superfluous bedclothes, an old light pulsing to the surface, and Jane could feel the urgency of it in her spine.

To Dream of the Dead

Rotherwas Chapel

Archaeologists are feeling this, too, in the wake of the finding of The Dinedor Serpent, or The Rotherwas Ribbon as it was originally and more prosaically called by local councillors who were wishing it would just curl up and die.

The subplot of *The Remains of an Altar* involved the discovery of ancient stones under a site in Coleman's Meadow, Ledwardine which Herefordshire Council had earmarked for development. In the book, this led to major protests, involving environmental, heritage and pagan factions, led, of course, by Jane Watkins.

Even as that book was being prepared for publication, archaeologists were uncovering what was described as a unique Bronze Age ritual construction ... right in the path of a new road planned by that same local authority.

It was almost uncanny, and there was no way I could get out of using the Dinedor Serpent in a future novel. Especially as it, too, generated a massive row, with the council accused of — literally — a cover-up in its determination to make sure the road went through.

Rotherwas Chapel

A man chained himself to a JCB and eight people were arrested for aggravated trespass for refusing to leave the council's HQ, where the issue was to be discussed in private. Because there weren't enough spare cells at Hereford, some of them were taken to Worcester, where they languished for hours. 'I spent the time psychically cleansing my cell,' one woman said.

In the end, all charges were dropped, but it left a nasty taste.

Rotherwas has not, in recent years, been the most favoured part of Hereford. Industrial estates — and Rotherwas has Hereford's biggest — are seldom scenic. The area's architectural jewel, Rotherwas Chapel, Elizabethan family chapel of the Catholic Bodenhams, is just round the corner from the public dump.

But the chapel, the dump and the factories all share the city's finest backdrop: Dinedor Hill, with its woodland and its Celtic camp.

And now the Dinedor Serpent, which the Council has always preferred to refer to as the Rotherwas Ribbon — far less sexy; who would ever want to visit that?

The new road (left) and myself (far right) standing alongside The Serpent 'path'

The Serpent

So ... what exactly is it, and why was it constructed?

Well, of course, we don't know.

It was found during a routine archaeological scan of the proposed site of the Rotherwas relief road — a planned shortcut out of the industrial estate.

There never was, to be honest, much to see.

In *To Dream of the Dead*, a councillor dismisses the Serpent as 'patio gravel'. Which, as you can see in the picture above (part of the Serpent is exposed behind me and the dowser Chris Hinsley — he's the one with the beard) is not entirely insulting.

The small stones are believed to be fire-cracked, the result of rocks dropped into a burning pit. The original theory was that they were then used for the surface of a path, some kind of ritual walkway possibly all the way from the top of Dinedor Hill to the River Wye. But the fact that there was no substructure suggested they weren't exactly for walking on.

Could they simply have been chippings thrown away after the stones had been used for some other purpose — the first industrial waste to be dumped at Rotherwas? But why were so many of the fragments found to be quartz?

Archaeologists began to consider the idea that because of the quartz content, likely to glow in the moonlight, the curving path could have been intended as some kind of Bronze Age special-effect, reflecting the meandering of the river. Awesome under a full moon.

Somehow, it answers all the criteria for an authentic spirit path, connecting the sacred river (rivers were seen as entrances to the otherworld) with Hereford's holy hill. Unsuitable for human beings, a point of access for the ancestors.

If it is a monument, the only comparable ones are the Serpent Mounds of Ohio, conserved at huge expense. As an American said, on hearing about Dinedor, 'We'd kill to have a find like that.'

In *To Dream of the Dead*, someone *is* killed, part of him displayed on the preaching cross near the ruins of the Blackfriars Monastery, which crouch behind the medieval Coningsby Hospital in Widemarsh Street.

In some cities the Blackfriars Monastery would be a major tourist attraction. In Hereford it's a secret. Wander in there, the chances are you'll be on your own. But at least it's conserved.

The future of the Serpent remains unclear. The road is now open. Archaeologists tended to agree that the only way of preserving the remains was to cover them up, but the bitter irony of having industrial traffic roaring over a possible ritual path has not gone unnoticed.

The day before *To Dream of the Dead* was published, the *Hereford Journal* published a reader's letter as a page lead under the headline

Look out for the curse
of the Dinedor Serpent

The letter more or less suggested that Hereford Council, by going ahead with the road out of Rotherwas, had opened up its own fast-track to hell ...

For many local people, the idea of hell is what the Council might have in mind for the green countryside now opened up by the road.

In *To Dream*, the parallels between the Serpent and the Coleman's Meadow excavation are underlined again.

This page and opposite:
Blackfriars Monastery Hereford

Climate change is coming to Ledwardine, as it has to many local villages which had never been flooded until the new millennium. Jane Watkins, mindful of Nick Drake's somehow sinister song *River Man*, attempts to communicate with the worryingly swelling river which for, as long as anyone can remember, has been seeping sluggishly under the bridge at Ledwardine but is now getting greedy.

Meanwhile, a corporate chill hangs over the city of Hereford, where the felling of town-centre trees and the closure of local businesses, including the city's best and friendliest department store, Chadd's, signals a slippage into what Frannie Bliss, of Hereford CID, calls Landfill Britain.

To Dream of the Dead reflects the spread of a new unease in modern Hereford as its distant past is revealed.

Further investigations in Rotherwas have uncovered indications of more extensive prehistoric settlement. Meanwhile, the county's first henge has been discovered in the Lugg Valley.

Ancient Herefordshire has been neglected. The current thinking is that this area was far more important in the Neolithic world than was previously assumed. At present, its most prominent prehistoric monuments are Arthur's Stone, a burial chamber near Dorstone visited by

This page and opposite: Arthur's Stone

Jane and her boyfriend Eirion in *The Remains of an Altar*, the Queen Stone in the Wye Valley and the Wern Derys standing stone, near Michaelchurch Escley, pictured on the cover of *To Dream of the Dead*.

The title of which comes from an old saying noted by Ella Mary Leather in *The Folklore of Herefordshire*:

To Dream of the Dead is a sign of rain.

How would anyone come up with a saying like that?

Only on the Border ...

Wern Derys

The Queen Stone, Huntsham

12   Gods of War

A treasure house. Out here in the deep sticks it was all so entirely
unexpected as to be approaching the surreal.

The Secrets of Pain

Stories in the Merrily Watkins series usually start with the location. Initially, this one seemed unpromising.

At the core of *The Secrets of Pain* is the SAS, so that meant the flat countryside around Credenhill, an untidy village getting slowly sucked into Hereford City, as new roads and the new livestock market open up development potential. An area which tourists cruise past in search of the more obviously scenic and historic.

But those flat, empty fields alongside the A438 — the Brecon Road — host the ghosts that William Wordsworth saw.

> While poring Antiquarians search the ground
> Upturned with curious pains, the Bard, a Seer,
> Takes fire: – The men that have been reappear;
> Romans for travel girt, for business gowned;
> And some recline on couches, myrtle gowned,
> In festal glee: why not?

This lesser-known poem is entitled simply

ROMAN ANTIQUITIES DISCOVERED AT BISHOPSTONE, HEREFORDSHIRE

and was written while the poet was staying with his wife's cousin, Thomas Hutchinson, who was leasing the 14th-century Brinsop Court, a mile or so outside Credenhill. Wordsworth first visited the Court in 1827 and planted a tree that still stands outside the house. Brinsop Church, about which more later, has a stained glass window in his memory.

Not many people know this. I didn't. Nor did I know much about the Romans in Herefordshire, because there really isn't much to see. The little shrine near the entrance to the National Trust Weir Gardens, a

The windows to William (above left) and Dorothy Wordsworth (above right) at Brinsop Church, and (below) a view up the Wye at Weir Gardens, the site of a Roman villa

handful of miles to the west, is not much more than a hole in the ground. Although the gardens offer some of the most interesting views of the River Wye west of Symonds Yat, the best of Roman Hereford is long gone.

Magnis, later known as Kenchester, was a substantial Roman town built close to the sacred River Wye on the route from Caerleon to Chester. In the 1st century AD, it had streets of shops and industrial buildings and suburban homes. Most of the stonework was plundered over the centuries for church buildings and the foundations of the new city growing a few miles away. 'Of the decay of Kenchester,' wrote John Leland, the Tudor antiquarian, 'Hereford rose and flourished.' But there was still plenty to see when William Stukeley checked it out towards the end of the 18th century:

The possible Roman shrine near the entrance to the gardens at the Weir

> A very fine mosaic floor a few years ago was found intire, soon torn to pieces by the ignorant and vulgar. I took up some remaining stones of different colours, and several bits of fine potter's ware of red earth … All around the city you may easily trace the walls, some stones being left everywhere, though overgrown by hedges and timber trees.

Interestingly, the most significant discoveries were made while *The Secrets of Pain* was being written, in 2010. The construction of the Yazor Brook Flood Alleviation Scheme meant that rescue-archaeologists were allowed into the Credenhill area ahead of the contractors. Significant Roman remains were soon unearthed, including the one that made the *Daily Mail*:

Archaeologists find 'muscular' body of British 'female gladiator'
Archaeologists have uncovered the remains of a 'massive, muscular woman' who may have been a female gladiator during the Roman occupation of Britain.

The woman was buried in an elaborate wooden coffin with iron straps and copper strips in Credenhill, Herefordshire — close to the headquarters of the SAS.

Her remains were found in a crouched position in an area thought to be a suburb of the nearby Roman town of Kenchester.

Archaeologists swiftly denied that there was any evidence that the woman had been a star of the arena, although it did give me an idea for a modern character of similar build called Victoria Buckland. The Roman history used in *The Secrets of Pain* was, however, strongly male-oriented, because *Magnis* began as a military base. 'A landscape quietly dedicated to war', is how the area is described to Merrily Watkins and Lol Robinson.

And of course it still is. On the edge of vanished *Magnis*, in a fork made by two Roman roads, lies an unassuming assembly of huts, served by a network of new roads. A substantial military village, with high wire fences and armed guards, this former RAF base is now the headquarters of the Special Air Service.

The SAS, formed during the Second World War, was and is an elite fighting force, highly trained to operate secretly behind enemy lines. It's responsible for many of the modern Hereford legends. In *Who Dares Wins*, his official biography of The Regiment, Tony Geraghty quotes an SAS instructor:

> 'One moment the world is a nice place, calm and quiet and beautiful.
> The next moment it is bloody chaos and you are going to die unless
> you react with total outright violence.'

From this came the soundbite from Syd Spicer which burns itself into Merrily's consciousness.

> '... when you know that a difficult situation can only be resolved by an
> act of swift, efficient, intense and quite colossal violence.'

Syd, who first appeared in *The Remains of an Altar*, is an ex-SAS man turned clergyman, as some do. No big surprise. Tony Geraghty remarks that the SAS has its own kind of mysticism.

He also notes that 'for some it is the living on after the action that requires the final reserves of courage'.

Which led me, inevitably, to *Baptism of Fire*, the autobiography of Frank Collins, the SAS man who was there in the Regiment's most public moments — when live TV tracked the Operation Nimrod team's arrival on the roof of the Iranian embassy to liberate nineteen hostages.

Frank Collins later became, like Syd Spicer, a clergyman — curate, for a time, at St Peter's, Hereford, before rejoining the Army as a chaplain. He was forced to resign after failing to obtain permission to publish *Baptism of Fire*, which reveals some of the more disturbing aspects of life in the Regiment. The SAS often creates stronger ties than a family, and the resulting depression probably led to his suicide in 1998.

A significant quote from Frank Collins's book found its way into *The Secrets of Pain*.

> 'They're all mad in one way or another. There's Kev, who knows he's
> a reincarnated Viking. There's Si, who only reads books about the
> paranormal ... Only a few of the boys are normal, but they're so normal
> they're weird. What a bunch of crazies we are. And we go out with our
> lethal weapons every day.'

Obviously, I've met a few SAS men, but I didn't consult any of them directly about the developments in *Secrets*. A source close to the Regiment said, 'They like all the novels and the sensationalism. It adds to the mystique, and the mystique is very important. All they don't like is leaks ...'.

I'm not aware of any SAS men following the particular channel of paganism explored in *Secrets*, but another highly-informed source said, 'Wouldn't surprise me at all.' So that was all right.

'It's been read ... at the Camp,' I was told quietly, a few weeks after the book came out.

The SAS, it seems, likes a landscape moulded for defence. The Regiment's first base was near Dinedor Hill on the edge of Hereford City. Today, Credenhill's wooded flank forms its eastern horizon — another fortified hill, once the biggest Iron Age camp in Herefordshire, now a country park, with scenic walks. Not far from its base is the hamlet of Brinsop, with its 14th-century Court and a fascinating little church, which proved to be not only another significant component of the *Secrets* story but probably the central one.

On the outside, it looks quite modest, on its own, next to a field of sheep and lambs. Plain and solid, like a mid-Wales church, no steeple, just a small belltower. One of its biggest gravestones is the memorial to William and Dorothy Wordsworth's employee, Jane Winder, who travelled with them and died at Brinsop.

One of the paths around the Iron Age fort at Credenhill

But the elevated churchyard suggests that the medieval church replaced a more rudimentary pre-Christian place of worship. You can imagine a circle of stones here, overlooking the very old moat which you can still see between the churchyard and the forestry at the foot of Credenhill. The humps in the higher land behind the church suggest there was once a substantial village, but now the only other nearby structure is in the sheep field below.

This is the Dragon's Well.

A stile gives access to the squat stone and a drain cover concealing the well. This dragon is the monster serpent reportedly slain by the patron saint of England, St George, and this where the confrontation is said to have occurred.

George and the Dragon are all over Brinsop. Inside the church, early 20th-century embellishments by Sir William Comber show the traditional George as a knight in armour, his lance, typically, down the dragon's throat.

But on an early-medieval Romanesque tympanum, now on a wall of the nave, he's seen as a Roman soldier — more fitting, because this church is on the edge of Roman Hereford, and the carvings on this stone suggest another explanation, which is explored in the novel.

*Images of St George at Brinsop Church: on a banner, in stained glass,
in a Romanesque tympanum and as a statue*

Yazor Church

Brinsop Church

Kinnersley Church

Credenhill Church

On the wall beside the doorway you can see the mistily poignant remains of a mural: the Crucifixion, picking up on another theme from *Secrets*. It makes the Comber stuff look a little glitzy.

There's no monument here — or anywhere — to the great Alfred Watkins, unless you include the church itself and the other three of medieval (and probably earlier) origins — Mansell Lacy, Yazor and Kinnersley — which form a clear straight line through Brinsop to the mother hill behind.

Mansell Lacy Church

In the City of Hereford, the last home of Alfred Watkins near the Cathedral is linked by a narrow alleyway to East Street, where, in *The Secrets of Pain*, a double murder is linked to the fruit farms whose polytunnels lie like worm casts in the fields around *Magnis*.

The Lol Robinson song, *The Simple Trackway Man*, on the CD, *A Message from the Morning*, is dedicated to AW.

I am a simple trackway man
As walks the lanes by ancient plan
Leading the people from beacon to steeple
And steeple to stone
And all the way home.

East Street, Hereford. Alfred Watkins' last house lies behind the buildings on the left

13 The Keys to the Kingdom

It was nearing midnight, a waxing moon and stars on show – not
much light-pollution from Hay, no traffic, no people. When
Gwenda's bar had closed and his drinking companions had gone
home, Robin had walked the empty sloping streets, up and down
stone steps, across cobbles, for over an hour, intent on clearing his
head. But his head had only filled up with the town. Starting with
the gothic clocktower, starlit, moonlicked, a fairytale touch ...

The Magus of Hay

*A modern sculpture to a
king high on a wall by
Hay's market square*

Hay-on-Wye: you really couldn't make it up ... but let's try.

There's this small agricultural town on the edge of Mid Wales, economi-
cally-challenged like most of them, which decides to start farming secondhand
books.

Within a few years, it has around forty bookshops.

And a King.

The King is Richard Booth, pioneer of the Hay booktrade. He has a crown
with jewels taken from a fancy dog-collar. He has a robe with fake ermine, and
he carries an orb made from a lavatory ballcock.

People laugh at King Richard. But not for long.

Hay sits right on the Border, just inside Wales but with a Herefordshire postal
address that fools Midland TV news editors into thinking it's in their patch.

Even before his coronation, Richard Booth had decided Hay should be
independent of both Wales and England. The Wales Tourist Board and the
Development Board for Rural Wales should be banned from the town, along
with national supermarkets and chainstores. Local councils should, wherever
possible, be ignored.

'Hay-on-Wye is the first town in the British Isles which has expressed its
intention of declaring independence from the bureaucratic control of Central

107

Government,' the King announced. He was wearing his robes and crown and puffing on a forearm-length Mexican cigar. His Cabinet, in jeans and scruffy sweaters, posed for the media, while a journalist asked the King if he was serious.

'Of course not,' he said. 'But it's more serious than real politics.'

And so it proved.

Soon, Hay was attracting book-tourists from all over the world, had become the most successful small town in the whole of Wales. The country's most famous inland resort.

And it was nothing to do with The Establishment.

The quangos (quasi-autonomous non-government organisations) had indeed somehow been shut out. There were no chainstores — even Boots the chemist soon disappeared, leaving Hay to Jones the local chemist's. The only supermarket — the Co-op — is, as it happens, just over the English border.

More booksellers moved in. Local people who might not otherwise have become booksellers found a new vocation. Individual supportive businesses — a greengrocer's, a rural delicatessen, a handful of new eateries — began to appear between the bookshops. Some also sold books — you can even find a few in the venerable jewellers', Mayalls — as if books have become a necessary talisman, a lucky charm.

Building on Hay's international reputation, a book festival, which began in a small way around the pubs in the town, became the biggest event of its kind in the country, bringing in tens of thousands of visitors and attracting the world's most famous writers, as well as leading politicians, musicians and movie stars. One year it included both Bill Clinton and Paul McCartney.

It was like a fairy tale, and in the tradition of fairy tales, the King bought Hay Castle and moved in thousands of secondhand books — books having already filled up the former fire station and the former cinema. A thriving economy had grown out of what can only be

described as a modern myth. A legend. A piece of contemporary folklore. It's difficult to think of anything similar happening anywhere else, ever.

It was as though Richard Booth's inspired move had attracted a strange kind of energy. As though some kind of independence had, on some level, actually occurred.

This little grey-brown town between the Black Mountains and the River Wye had acquired a strangely exotic ambience. Something slightly magical about it.

Which gave me the central idea for *The Magus of Hay*.

The Castles

It's not easy setting a novel — particularly a thriller — in a real place, with a story that involves real, living people. You can't put words into the mouths of people who know that you know they didn't utter them.

But you can have your characters talking about real people, operating around them. And you can risk a possible small walk-on part for the King himself, just to show that, like the castle on the cover of *The Magus of Hay*, he actually exists.

Hay Castle is a mongrel, with a Norman gateway and the remains of a Jacobean mansion and some Victorian bits and ... you get the idea. Windsor Castle just wouldn't work in Hay.

Hay Castle

The Magus of Hay never goes inside the castle. There's no need to. But it's there as a living symbol of medieval Hay and a legacy of violence that not everyone in this novel wants to forget.

Your best source book for the early medieval history of Hay Castle is actually a novel, Barbara Erskine's *Lady of Hay*, published in 1986. This is the story of a woman hypnotically regressed into the persona of Mathilda — sometimes called Maud — who is said to have built the castle. Mathilda was married to William de Braose, the archetypal Norman baron who ran this part of the border in the days of King John. Like his king, de Braose, who has a historical role in *The Magus of Hay*, was not always portrayed as a bad guy, but mostly he was. What matters more in *Magus* is how he's perceived.

Back in the 20th century, things didn't always go right for King Richard. The Booth business sometimes teetered on the brink of bankruptcy, and a good part of the castle was destroyed by fire, apparently started by a large rogue log in the hearth. But even that's a part of tradition on the Welsh border, where most castles have been torched and plundered at one time or another.

As this was the first novel explicitly about Hay since Barbara Erskine's book, which also involves the paranormal, I wanted a title that didn't sound like *Lady of Hay*. My first idea was *The Turning of Hay*, which I thought had a nice agricultural feel while also echoing Henry James' classic ghost story, *The Turn of the Screw*. Unfortunately nobody at the publishing end liked it, and the only other title I came up with that they did like was *The Magus of Hay*.

Hay Castle gateway and keep, from the outside (this page) and from the bailey (opposite)

The narrow end of Back Fold

Barbara says she doesn't mind.

The late, great Rob Soldat, historian and folklorist and himself a medieval-looking figure on the streets of Hay, told me some stories about the castle, including one about a bloodstain that wouldn't go away — a story which, in the end, I didn't use because my novel never needed to go inside. What was important was that the castle was there, crowning the town, frowning over the market place.

The streets of old Hay curl up from the bank of the River Wye to the castle's curtain walls. If you look at a street plan, you can seen they form the shape of a heart. I've examined it on several maps and Google Earth, and the heart is always apparent. The castle isn't part of it.

Closest to the castle is the alleyway known as Back Fold, home to George Greenway's bookshop and Haydn Pugh's Juke Joint, next to which, in the novel, sit Jeeter Kapoor's cricket bookshop and Thorogoods' Pagan Books. But before the shops

were here, Back Fold was the home of the castle's abattoir, and the tradition of slaughter continued until relatively recently.

Interestingly, Hay once had two castles. Of the other, far smaller one, only the mound remains, down near the parish church. We don't really know when or why it was abandoned and why the big castle was built much further away from the river, which must have been far more important to Hay then than it is now.

The River

The Wye is surely the most revered river in southern Britain, but in Hay, you really have to search for it. Even the road bridge crossing the river from old Breconshire to old Radnorshire is the least-obvious road out of town. And in the town itself, I'm fairly sure, there are no signs pointing to the water's edge. Like Builth Wells, the next town upriver, Hay has turned its back on the Wye. To get a glimpse of it from the town, you need to climb up to the castle.

The best actual riverside walk leads from a footpath between the old castle mound and the parish church, past a waterfall and a scenic gorge, to where the old railway ran until it was ripped up following the infamous Beeching purge.

Alongside the path to the river (above) and waterfalls high up Cusop Dingle (below)

Turn left and you come to the Warren, a public field open to the river and the Radnorshire hills. Turn right and you follow the bank to the new bridge, beyond which is the sewage works, where a stream trickles discreetly into the river by a small pebble beach. You can actually reach this place from a track at the other end of the town (turn left before the vets' clinic). There's a small car park, stepping down to green banks and the little beach and the mouth of the aforementioned humble stream. This is the Dulas Brook, far more important than it looks, because it marks the actual boundary between Wales and England, rushing down from a place called ...

Cusop

A mysterious place in England, just. And although fields and the Dulas Brook divide them, well-wooded Cusop, with its big, dark houses, is virtually a suburb of Hay. King Richard's family home is here, and Herbert Rowse Armstrong, the famous Hay poisoner

Cusop Church (above and below)

— the only solicitor ever actually hanged for murder, as the King likes to point out , also lived in Cusop.

It's a village without a centre, only a terminus with an ancient church and a castle mound and folklore involving fairies and the Will-o'-the-Wisp, retold by Mrs Leather, who wrote in 1912:

Fairies have been seen dancing under foxgloves in Cusop Dingle within the memory of some now living there.

I was interested in the Will-o'-the-Wisp, a moving light effect, often said to attract travellers from the road and into the abyss. Years earlier, our neighbour, Ken Ratcliffe, who came from Cusop, had told me about the time he saw the whole landscape inexplicably lit up. Ken's wife, Jessie thought it might have been a UFO. But unexplained phenomena are not uncommon in Cusop.

Its lower half, the fairy-haunted Cusop Dingle, has a road that follows the Dulas Brook along the England/Wales border. Here, the brook is not the little stream that flows placidly into the big Wye by the Hay sewage works, but something more urgent and dramatic, with several waterfalls. The pool below one of the most dramatic of these, right next to the road, is deeper than it looks, and a man drowned there. Recently, since a car went over the edge, the pool has been caged by metal bars.

The low mound on which Cusop Castle stood is almost facing the church, which is partly Norman, possibly on the site of an earlier place of worship and is dedicated to St Mary. As is Hay Church. As is the little church up in the Black Mountains, beyond Hay Bluff, in the place called …

Cusop Castle mound

Capel-y-ffin

The chapel at the end. But the end of what?

St Mary's, Capel-y-ffin is actually a very small church, endearingly bent, reached by the mountain road which passes under Hay Bluff, alongside a not very impressive but certainly well-appointed prehistoric stone circle.

Hay Bluff is where, in the 1980s, the Convoy used to gather in the autumn — a chain of ancient buses, vans and ex-ambulances carrying the post-hippies who came in search of the magic mushrooms growing in quantity around the Bluff. The key ingredient of these tiny fungi is psilocybin which can promote visionary experiences and has recently been described as better than Prozac, if less legal. A member of the Convoy once presented me with a bag of mushrooms which, he said, should be dried, crushed and brewed like tea, but I wimped out.

Part of the stone circle at the foot of Hay Bluff

Looking along the ridge of the Black Mountains above Hay. Hay Bluff is just off to the left; Gospel Pass passes through the cleft in the ridge

The church at Capel-y-ffin

The Convoy were themselves a mixed bag, including romantics in search of a spiritual retreat, anarchists looking for a revolution and — let's not dress this up — a few itinerant thieves. New Age Travellers was the term they preferred, citing gypsy-rules when making yet another appearance at Talgarth Magistrates' Court, where they were represented by an amiable traveller who came into court wearing a black suit and carrying a stack of law books. He never really won, but it was fun while it lasted, and the Convoy slipped into history as part of a long tradition of eccentrics attracted to this corner of the Black Mountains.

Towards the end of the 19th century, the scattered farmers of Capel-y-ffin had watched, faintly baffled, as a band of robed monks arrived to build a monastery under the direction of a man seen by some as a living saint.

Joseph Leycester Lyne was an Anglican deacon, healer and visionary who had become obsessed with founding an Anglo-Catholic monastic community by refurbishing the scenic ruins of Llanthony Priory, lower down the valley. He'd toured Britain, raising the money through talks and healing sessions, but finally had to admit that modernising Llanthony was always going to be beyond him.

And so, under his working name of Father Ignatius, he switched his ambitions a few miles to a wooded hillside at Capel-y-ffin, a place whose wild, yet numinous qualities appealed to him at once. The neo-gothic

The ruins of Llanthony Priory

monastery can be seen to this day, alongside Fr Iggy's church, which was not so well-built, and under which, eventually, he was buried, leaving the church to become a ruin.

Dismissed by many as a charlatan and exalted as an 'untiring sower of the seed divine' in the not entirely impartial biography by Beatrice, Baroness of Bertouche, Fr Ignatius was nationally famous in his day and is now virtually forgotten. His miracles — including the raising of a builder crushed to death by a pile of building stone — are regarded with a certain scepticism. Nonetheless, setting up a working monastery at a place like Capel-y-ffin

The ruins of Father Ignatius' church

was some achievement, and he did leave behind a mystery which puts the Black Mountains alongside Lourdes, Knock and Medjugorje.

Capel-y-ffin monastery, now used as a Youth Hostel

The Lady of Llanthony

Beatrice de Bertouche is probably right when she says that, in a Catholic country, these phenomena would have been commemorated by 'some costly shrine'.

All we have at Capel is a touchingly-frayed modern statue of the Virgin Mary, now planted in front of Fr Iggy's monastery which has been used, of late, as a youth hostel and pony-trekking centre.

She's been moved, probably for her own safety, from the more exposed spot in a nearby field where, in the late summer of 1880, it all began to happen.

On the evening of Monday, August 30th, four choirboys were playing cricket, using a stick, in the Abbot's Meadow when one of them, John Stewart, 12, spotted what Beatrice describes as a dazzling figure gliding across the field.

> The form was of a woman, a veil hung over the head and face, the hands were both raised as if in blessing.

And, very slowly, it was coming towards them.

Thomas Foord, 11, was not happy about this.

'If it comes near me I'll hit it with my stick,' he's reported to have said.

The Holy Mother, it seems, took the hint and slid into the hedge, where she remained for a few moments before vanishing into a bush.

And it was this bush which, on subsequent occasions, was seen to be lit up when the countryside all around was in darkness.

One of the monks, Brother Dunstan, was among the later witnesses.

> We knelt opposite the bush but some distance from it and began to say prayers and sing hymns but no figure appeared. Presently, I suggested that if it was really the Blessed Virgin who had appeared to the boys on Monday, possibly if we sang the Ave Maria she might again appear. So we began to sing the Ave ... and at once perceived the form of a woman surrounded by light at the top of the meadow by the gate.

The apparitions were said to have continued for some time, varying from full figures to starry lights in the bush, leaves from which would go on, according to Beatrice, to bring about 'miraculous cures'.

A small chorus of dissent was led by Sister Marry Agnes who, as a nun at Capel, had been badly bullied by a particular Mother Superior. Sister Marry Agnes suggested that the visitations had been created by a magic lantern, which, it has to be said, seems like a serious overestimation of the power of those early projectors.

Still, you can imagine that an appearance by the Virgin Mary might well have been dreamed up by Father Ignatius as a way of attracting tourists and money but, if international fame was expected, it didn't happen. The Lady of Llanthony has been all but forgotten. Far more has been written about the man who occupied the monastery in the 1920s, long after the departure of the monks.

Eric Gill, who came over from England, was a famous sculptor, stone carver and designer of type-faces. He was also a devout Catholic, of the Roman persuasion, who established at Capel-y-ffin a small community, including his extended family, the Welsh painter David Jones and various priests brought in to celebrate the Mass in his private chapel.

All very pre-hippy, but there was a darker side. A biography by Fiona McCarthy, published in 1989, revealed that Eric Gill's spiritual yearnings were coupled with physical desires of what you might call an experimental nature. He had sexual relations with his daughters. And his dog, apparently.

How Eric felt about the Lady of Llanthony doesn't seem to be recorded anywhere, but he fitted well into a pattern of unorthodox religious behaviour that I was beginning to detect in this area of the Border.

It seemed not unreasonable to suggest, in *The Magus of Hay*, that another mystical community had existed near Capel-y-ffin in the 1980s, and that, because of its proximity to the town of books, it should attract some of the writers who increasingly converged on Hay.

An obvious one was the travel writer and novelist Bruce Chatwin, who spent a lot of time in the Black Mountains where he set his novel *On the Black Hill*. His fictional town of Rhulen, its name borrowed from a hamlet on the edge of Radnor Forest, is thought to have been based on Hay-on-Wye. Bruce Chatwin was a well-known freeloader, often borrowing people's houses to write in, notably Scethrog Tower, near Brecon, the 14th-century home of the jazz-singer, writer and journalist George Melly.

Jeremy Sandford, who wrote the seminal TV plays Cathy Come Home and Edna the Inebriate Woman, lived in nearby Herefordshire, was a friend of the King of Hay, championed gypsies and travellers generally and wrote a book called *In Search of Magic Mushrooms*.

There's no record of the distinguished novelist Dame Beryl Bainbridge ever spending time at Capel-y-ffin, as she does in the novel, though it did seem the sort of thing she might do. I only met Beryl a couple of times – at the Hay Festival, as it happened – but she was always there in the background, since the days after my first novel, *Candlenight*, was discovered by her editor and friend, Anna Haycraft, who wrote as Alice

Thomas Ellis. Dame Beryl's spiritual beliefs were uncertain, but her Anglo-Catholic funeral is legendary, and she just seemed to float naturally into *Magus*.

Meanwhile, down in Hay itself, the torch of Anglo-Catholicism had been reignited in the new millennium.

Mary's return

Capel-y-ffin, Llanthony, and eventually Abergavenny, are linked to Hay by the tortuous mountain road known as the Gospel Pass, so called because two prominent Apostles are said to have taken this route on a rare (extremely rare) visit to the British Isles.

Like the Malverns, which they face across Herefordshire, the Black Mountains have a long history of mysterious worship, Christian and pagan. But few people would have expected the air in Hay Church to be laden with the scent of incense again, so long after the Reformation.

Anglo-Catholicism has been a triumph for Father Richard Williams who, in an age of falling congregations, has more than tripled the turn-out at St Mary's. A tabernacle stands on the altar, guarded by a collection of candlelit figurines. Across from the votive stand is a painted Virgin and child. And the Mass is back. More Catholic, say some of the expanded flock, than most RC churches.

The church at Hay (this page and opposite)

In the tradition of eccentricity without which Hay would be just another rural, market town, Fr Richard's curate was his standard poodle, Jimmy, who attended services along with any other dogs that happened to turn up with their owners.

It's the same at his other churches, at Llanigon and, of course Capel-y-ffin, about which Fr Richard wrote in his parish magazine:

> ... artists, poets and visionaries have found this place a place where 'Prayer is valid' ... where the veil between the visible world and the invisible has worn diaphanously thin.

Even Fr Richard is a little sceptical about some of the legends of Fr Ignatius, but he doesn't dismiss the sightings of the Lady of Llanthony. For him, too, the story is given a certain substance by the anecdote about the choirboy and the stick.

You may well be hearing more, in the future, about the Virgin of the Black Mountains.

Hitler in the hills?

Fr Richard and Merrily Watkins are not in the same diocese, but neither Hereford nor Swansea-and-Brecon has a tradition of Anglo-Catholicism. Other ministers, in both dioceses, seem to take a dim view of what's happening in Hay. But, as we've seen, the Border country is good at breaking down barriers and making its own rules.

Also, there's always been a strong element of paganism in the border hills, some of it quite close to Christianity, as reflected by the Sheelagh-na-gig and green man ornaments in so many churches. But, at various times, there have also been signs of something radically opposed to Christianity, wilfully embracing shadows.

Nicholas Goodrick-Clarke's authoritative book, *Black Sun*, has a long chapter on extreme right-wing groups practising magic on the Welsh Border in the 1980s and '90s, and the Internet is still loaded with fascist philosophical ramblings by one or two people living around Herefordshire, Shropshire and Powys.

Goodrick-Clarke suggested these attitudes had formed out of the search for self-sufficiency which brought hundreds of good-lifers into the border hills in the 1970s. It's not difficult to imagine a few of them sharing the beliefs of the survivalists and white-supremacists in remote areas of the US. *Black Sun* suggests that Saxon and Nordic forms of paganism and the magical beliefs of Himmler's SS came together in areas of Herefordshire, Shropshire and Powys in the late 20th century, with ceremonies at prehistoric sites and hints of blood sacrifice. The extent of this belief-system remains uncertain, but some of its followers — who regarded Hitler as an avatar or demi-god heralding a new era of violent ethnic cleansing in the West — do seem to be still around.

The family of William Joyce — the Nazi radio propagandist Lord Haw Haw — is said to have had links to Hay, and the Mosleyite Lord Brocket, apparently a guest at Hitler's birthday party, was up the road, for a time, at Kinnersley Castle. There were also rumours that the right-wing Lord Lucan was accommodated in the area while on the run following the murder of his children's nanny.

All far removed from the friendly, chaotic regime of independent Hay, in Liberal-Democrat Brecon and Radnor, but everybody dreams, and some dreams are dark.

The future

The future for Hay is as blurred as the Lady of Llanthony.

A brain tumour caused a dramatic hiatus in Richard Booth's roller-coaster career and the progress of Independent Hay. He recovered, he's back ... but times have changed.

The town is now well-established as an inland resort and tourist haven and the Castle, now in the hands of a local trust, is being revived as a centre for the arts. Richard's principal bookshop, The Limited, is in new hands, looks a good deal less eccentric, but is still trading as Richard Booth's Bookshop. But several secondhand bookshops, as well as the only purveyor of new books, have closed down in the past few years, victims of the Recession, the national decline of the high-street and, of course, the rise of the e-book which means that far fewer books are now unobtainable and fewer people need to haunt the secondhand shops in search of some elusive title. Long-time bookseller Derek Addyman, who recently acceded to the title of Prince of Hay, declared war on the new devices, and the cover of *The Kindle Crack'd from Side to Side* by Agatha Addyman appeared in the window of the Murder and Mayhem bookshop.

There had been other tensions over the years: ambitious outsiders who wanted a piece of Hay, and – because Richard Booth wasn't really in charge — sometimes got one.

And success, too, had its inevitable downside for some people. Property prices went through the roof and local young people were forced out as wealthy incomers arrived, lured by the idea of a cultural haven in a comparatively remote area.

Again, this probably would not have happened if the King had possessed real power — Richard Booth made a point of employing local people and, as Gomer Parry points out, 'sometimes we even got paid'.

And some of the incomers were eccentric enough to fit in. I'm not going to name them; they know who they are. They're characters looking for a novel.

But, as you can't have too many real people in a novel, for *The Magus of Hay* I had to re-populate the town with a parallel cast of refugees who would fit the ethos. And if you find it hard to separate fact from fiction ... you'll know you're finally starting to understand Hay.

14   The Others

> Lying low, at the centre of the well-tamed land, snug as a ground-nesting bird, was this bright and modern country settlement, its buildings elegantly structured with red brick and new timber framing. I marked a proud, towered church with a flag of St George. And sensed a glow about the place ...
>
> *The Heresy of Dr Dee*

> When Jack went to ring the old bell, he walked alone. Nobody else on the streets, the town holding its breath, even the sagging old buildings seeming to tense their timbers.
>
> *Curfew*

Actually, before this was Merrily's Border, it was Gomer Parry country. And before that — four centuries before — it was Dee country.

Gomer made his first appearance in 1992, in my second novel, *Crybbe*, now republished as *Curfew*.

Looking back, this was quite an influential story. It was, to be honest, designed as a British answer to Stephen King, who has, over the years, inflicted all kinds of alien horrors on the US state of Maine, where he lives, prompting several other American writers to import elements of English and Welsh folklore into the New World. Occasionally, it worked. More often than not it made you wince.

So *Curfew* brings together many of the mysteries — British mysteries, in situ — relating to prehistoric monuments, mainly standing stones, circles and burial mounds. It's the story of a small town on the Welsh Border chosen as a centre for New Age research by an Australian entrepreneur who wants to restore the ancient stones that once surrounded it and falls foul of local people who know things he doesn't.

There isn't, as far as I know, a town anywhere in Radnor or Herefordshire that was ever inside a stone circle, in the way of, say, the village of Avebury, in Wiltshire. But most of Crybbe's other peculiarities were drawn from established legends and real features, notably

The Curfew

Crybbe is not entirely based on Presteigne — think also Knighton, Bishops Castle and Clun – but, well, mostly it is.

Presteigne, though in Wales and once the county town of Radnorshire, lies on the English side of the border earthwork Offa's Dyke. With its crooked timber-framed buildings and medieval air, it seems very olde English, sometimes merrie, sometimes less so.

This is the town with the curfew, established in 1565 by John Beddoes, the Elizabethan wool merchant after whom the local high school would be named. The curfew bell is in the tower of the parish church, and a sum of money — the income from the lease of local fields — was left by John Beddoes to ensure that it would always be rung every night.

When, some years ago, its future was threatened, the musician Mike Oldfield who lived near Kington for some years, stepped in with the money. The fact that music from Oldfield's Tubular Bells had been the theme of The Exorcist did not go unnoticed — well, not by me, anyway.

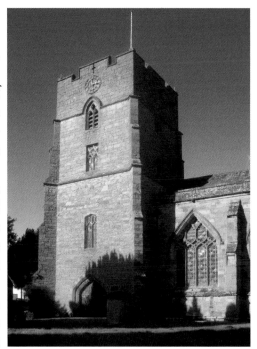

The belltower at Presteigne Church

The story retold in *Curfew*, about a dark force in the form of a hound coming down from an ancient mound into the town, echoes an experience related, in a radio programme I made, by the licensee of a pub in Presteigne who was terrified by a howling at the bottom of the stairs in the night, when there was nothing there. She said her own West Highland terrier had, uncharacteristically, hidden under the bed. There were also fears that a previous landlady, who died after an unexplained fall from an upstairs window, had wanted to make an urgent exit from the premises at night.

There are, of course, other strange stories in Presteigne, where, during the 1980s, the resident policeman was also the local wart-charmer. It makes perfect sense that the family of a famous Elizabethan astrologer and magician should have lived not far away.

Dr Dee

Of all the Elizabethan heroes, John Dee is the most undersung. Recognised all over Europe as a brilliant mathematician by his early twenties, his reputation in Britain has always been discoloured by his experiments with magic.

Magic, of course, is what science used to be called in the days when it was linked with religion. John Dee sought to chart the dimensions of creation and know the mind of God — nothing too ambitious. His friend and former pupil, Robert Dudley, later Earl of Leicester, asked him to forecast a fortuitous day for the coronation of the new queen, which he did, and was consulted by her on matters of the Hidden for the rest of her long reign. Unlike Drake, Raleigh & co., however, he was never given a title and never made much money.

John was born in London, his father, Rowland Dee, having moved there from the family home, Nant-y-groes, near Pilleth, a few miles out of Presteigne.

The Heresy of Dr Dee takes John back to his roots in search of the Wigmore Shewstone, a famous crystal through which he believed he might catch celestial rays and raise his own consciousness to a level which could allow him to communicate with angelic forces. Which, in those days, was very much science.

The shewstone is based on an actual crystal which, for some time, was owned by the Harley family of Brampton Bryan. Nobody seems to know where it is now, but the Dee home, Nant-y-groes, can certainly still be seen. There are two houses there now, a farmhouse and a larger dwelling, expanded in Victorian times, on the other side of the lane from Whitton.

Pilleth Church

Both face Pilleth Hill, site of the battle in which a couple of thousand English soldiers were slain by the army of Owain Glyndwr and his general Rhys Gethin. Bones of the victims were still turning up on the hill in recent years, and memories of it were still painfully fresh in the 1560s when, in *The Heresy of Dr Dee*, Dee and Dudley arrive in Presteigne. Pilleth Church, which overlooks the novel's bloody climax, was burned down by the Welsh, then rebuilt and now has a strangely cheerful air. It was here, allegedly, that John's grandfather, Bedo Dee, had his son baptised in wine.

At Wigmore Abbey I discovered Abbot John Smart, a notorious wheeler-dealer who would undoubtedly have got along well with the renowned TV secondhand car dealer, Ambrose Boyce, as played by John Challis, who now lives there. It was John and his wife Carol who introduced me to Smart, who was involved in sundry fiddles and property deals and was not big on chastity. A man just demanding to be in the novel, so he is.

Although John Dee never makes it to Wigmore in *Heresy*, he actually did find his way there about ten years later to search the remains of Wigmore Castle for old books and documents to add to his famous library. Dee's diaries — at least the ones that have been found — make no mention of him returning to his family home, but it seems unlikely that he didn't. And there's a period, during his early 30s, when his biographers have been unable to discover what he was up to. It seemed reasonable for me to try and fill in the gaps, with reference to what was happening in England at the time.

But what did John Dee look like in those days? The only portraits show him as middle aged or elderly, and these have tended to condition the public perception of him as an old wizard, maybe Head of Maths at Hogwarts. I needed a picture of a younger man to work with, so I asked the graphic designer Bev Craven if he could take the most famous portrait of Dee, darken the hair, lose the white beard and ... well, here he is at thirty-three, still a little wary, even paranoid, but then he had cause to be.

December ...

... the other novel set on the Welsh Border, takes us back to Llanthony Priory, the medieval monastery which Fr Ignatius could never afford to restore.

This scenic ruin at the southern end of the Black Mountains was the model for the sinister abbey of Ystrad Ddu (every stone cemented in blood) in a story which turned the small hotel built into one corner of the ruins into a recording studio.

In December, a group of musicians falls victim to bad things linked to the famous Christmas massacre at Abergavenny Castle perpetrated by the Norman baron William de Braose (also of Hay Castle fame) in a bid to suppress Welsh opposition. The novel expands the legend of the harp-player who was supposed to have escaped the massacre and, for reasons too complicated to explain here, introduces the spectre of John Lennon. It also involves the Skirrid, the cleft peak near Abergavenny and one of the key turrets on the ramparts of the Hereford skyline, which is said to have split at the moment Jesus Christ died on the cross.

The classic picture of John Dee and the younger man 'exposed' by Bev Craven

The novel was out of print for several years but is now back in a new paperback from Corvus and an illustrated collector's edition from MHB.

There's also a full-length CD of music recorded at the Abbey by the band Philosopher's Stone, and remixed by Allan Watson, which takes the story a stage further. Abbey Tapes – the Exorcism is available through the website www.philrickman.co.uk. A full-length *December* audiobook read by Sean Barrett and including snatches of the music, is available from Isis.

The Merrily Watkins series (so far) with principal locations

The Wine of Angels	Ledwardine
Midwinter of the Spirit	Hereford
A Crown of Lights	The Radnor Valley
The Cure of Souls	The Frome Valley
The Lamp of the Wicked	Ross-on-Wye and the Forest of Dean
The Prayer of the Night Shepherd	Kington
The Smile of a Ghost	Ludlow
The Remains of an Altar	The Malverns
The Fabric of Sin	Garway
To Dream of the Dead	Ledwardine, Hereford
The Secrets of Pain	Hereford and Brinsop
The Magus of Hay	Hay-on-Wye

Also available are two full-length CDs, *Songs from Lucy's Cottage* and *A Message from the Morning*, by Lol Robinson with Hazey Jane II. A third relates to *December: Abbey Tapes, the Exorcism*, produced by Prof. Levin from the Abbey sessions. All available through the website, www.philrickman.co.uk and from I-tunes.

View over Ludlow from Whitcliffe Common

Select Bibliography

Richard Booth, *My Kingdom of Books* (Y Lolfa)

Mark Bowden, with David Field & Helen Winton, *The Malvern Hills, An ancient landscape* (English Heritage)

Paul Broadhurst, *The Green Man and the Dragon* (Mythos)

Bromyard and District Local History Society, *A Pocketful of Hops*

Ronald Bryer, *Not the Least, The Story of Little Malvern* (The Self-publishing Association)

Brian Cave, *The Countryside around Weston and Lea* (The Forest Bookshop)

Kate Clarke, *The Book of Hay* (Logaston Press)

Frank Collins, *Baptism of Fire* (Corgi)

Michael Cox, *M.R. James, An Informal Portrait* (Oxford)

  (Also strongly recommended: *The Ghosts and Scholars* magazine and online, edited by Rosemary Pardoe)

Paul Devereux, *Spirit Roads* (Collins & Brown)

                Haunted Land (Piatkus)

Tony Geraghty, *Who Dares Wins* (Warner books)

Pat Hughes and Heather Hurley, *The Story of Ross* (Logaston Press)

Michael Kennedy, *The Life of Elgar* (Cambridge)

  (Also well worth getting hold of Ken Russell's early BBC documentary on Elgar)

Ella Mary Leather, *The Folklore of Herefordshire* (Lapridge; currently out of print)

Patrick Jasper Lee, *We Borrow the Earth* (Thorsons)

David Lloyd, *The Concise History of Ludlow* (Merlin Unwin)

Les Lumsdon, *A Guide to Slow Travel in the Marches* (Logaston Press)

John Michell, *The View over Atlantis* (Garnstone, Abacus)

                The New View over Atlantis (Thames & Hudson)

                City of Revelation (Abacus)

Jerrold Northrop Moore, *Elgar, Child of Dreams* (Faber)

Roy Palmer, *Herefordshire Folklore* (Logaston Press)

                The Folklore of Radnorshire (Logaston Press)

                The Folklore of (old) Monmouthshire (Logaston Press)

Huw Parsons, *Planet Hay* (Peevish Bee Books)

Graham Roberts, *Around & About Herefordshire & the Southern Marches* (Logaston Press)

Ron Shoesmith, *Alfred Watkins — a Herefordshire Man* (Logaston Press; out of print)

Ron Shoesmith and Andy Johnson (editors) *Ludlow Castle* (Logaston Press)

Fred Slater, *The Nature of Central Wales* (Barracuda)

Rob Soldat, *A Walk around Hay* (Marches Vade Mecum)

Audrey Tapper, *Knights Templar and Hospitaller in Herefordshire* (Logaston Press)

Thomas Traherne, *Selected Poems and Prose* ed. Alan Bradford (Penguin)

Joan and Brian Thomas (and others), *Garway Hill Through the Ages* (Logaston Press)

Alfred Watkins, *The Old Straight Track*

Index

A corbel from Kilpeck Church